P9-BVH-899

GRUMMAN OV-1 MOHAWK

Developed during the late 1950s for battlefield reconnaissance, the OV-1 proved to be a valuable weapon during the Vietnam War. It provided field commanders with the answers to these questions: "Where are the enemy troops?" "How many are there?" "What are they doing?"

While the Mohawk never won any medals for speed or maneuverability, it was well-equipped for the job it was intended to do. It had all-weather navigation and communications equipment. It could land and take off on short runways. It offered its crew members at least some protection against ground fire.

The pilot sat on the left and an observer or equipment operator on the right. The multi-windowed cockpit gave both a commanding view of the battlefield.

The Mohawk could be equipped with a wide variety of reconnaissance gear. Often it carried a special camera that could take horizon-to-horizon photos. Other cameras could concentrate on smaller targets, such as road junctions, hamlets, or clusters of hills. The photographs provided the kind of detail that ground commanders needed.

The Mohawk could also be equipped with SLAR (Side-Looking Airborne Radar), which was housed in a long pod beneath the fuselage. The radar scanned roads used to bring troops and supplies into the battle area. A photographic map was produced from the radar signals while the plane was in flight, pinpointing targets for Air Force attack planes and gunships.

The Mohawk could also monitor battlefield equipment with infrared sensors. Any object—a chair, table, or coffee cup—gives off infrared rays, sometimes called heat rays. Sensing devices pick up infrared rays coming from various objects, and record the images of those objects on film. Like radar, infrared sensors can "see" at night in the dark or through fog. Infrared equipment proved especially valuable in Vietnam, because the North Vietnamese and Viet Cong often depended on darkness to conceal their movements.

OV-1 Mohawk is medium size—bigger and more powerful than light aircraft, yet smaller than four-engine planes.

JAPANESE CUISINE

FOR EVERYONE

PUBLISHER REPRESENTATIVE OFFICE

UNITED STATES: Prime Communication System
P.O. BOX 456 Shaw Island, WA 98286

AUTHOR'S SALES AGENCY: A.K. HARANO COMPANY
P.O. BOX 1022, Edmonds, WA 98020
Phone: (206) 774-5490
D & BH ENTERPRISES
94-443 Kahuanani Street, Waipahu, HI 96797
Phone: (808) 671-6041

OVERSEAS DISTRIBUTORS

UNITED STATES: JP TRADING, INC.
300 Industrial Way
Brisbane, Calif. 94005
Phone: (415) 468-0775, 0776

MEXICO: Publicaciones Sayrols, S.A. de C.V.

COLOMBIA: Jorge E. Morales & CIA LTDA.

TAIWAN: Formosan Magazine Press, Ltd.

HONG KONG: Apollo Book Company, Ltd.

THAILAND: Central Department Store Ltd.

SINGAPORE: MPH DISTRIBUTORS (S) PTE, LTD.

MALAYSIA: MPH DISTRIBUTORS SDN, BHD.

PHILIPPINES: National Book Store, Inc.

KOREA: Tongjin Chulpan Muyeok Co., Ltd.

INDONESIA: C.V. TOKO BUKU "MENTENG"

INDIA: Dani Book Land, Bombay 14

AUSTRALIA: BOOKWISE INTERNATIONAL

GUAM, SIPAN AND MICRONESIAN ISLANDS: FUJIWARA'S SALES & SERVICE

CANADA: MILESTONE PUBLICATIONS

UNITED STATES: MASA T. ASSOCIATES

First Edition April 1985, 16th Printing November 1997

Original Copyright © by Yukiko Moriyama

World rights reserved. Published by JOIE, INC. 1-8-3, Hirakawa-cho, Chiyoda-ku, Tokyo 102 Japan   Printed in Japan

No part of this book or portions thereof may be reproduced in any form or by any means including electronic retrieval systems without prior written approval from the author or publisher.

ISBN4-915249-20-4

ACKNOWLEDGMENTS

To the memory of my mother, who was always there when I needed help and who always gave immeasurable love.
To my father for his encouragement and understanding.

I would like to express my heartfelt gratitude to the following people for their invaluable assistance in making of "JAPANESE CUISINE FOR EVERYONE."

First, my special thanks are due to my publisher, Mr. Shiro Shimura for his trust and faith in my work.

Also to the following:
Photography: Seiichi Ishihara
Editorial Assistance: Akira Naito, Mieko Nagasawa, Etsuko Yamazaki, Carolyn Harano
Illustration: Michiko Hayashi, Mariko Suzuki
Kitchen Help: Eiko Ōishi, Yoshiko Morioka, Takako Sakata

Also I would like to give special thanks to my colleague Mr. Heihachiro Tohyama, co-author of "Sushi Cook Book," who was so generous in helping me with *Sashimi* and *Edomae-Sushi* for this book.

INTRODUCTION

Japanese cuisine, characterized by its natural taste and appearance has long been recognized as something delicious, elegant, and different.

Today, we have all come into closer contact with people of other countries, with their customs and traditions, and with foreign food through travel or advanced communication. Japanese cuisine is now attracting unprecedented world wide attention.

The Japanese are the world's leader as far as longevity is concerned. A lot of the traditional food eaten in Japan is from the sea and even today a great variety of fish is consumed daily. Japanese people have an affection for the sea, and what comes from the sea has always been valued and appreciated. In fact, most distinctive thing about Japanese cooking is the use of *kombu* (kelp), dried bonito flakes and small, dried sardines for the basic soup stock. These ingredients are used in other way as well. Soybean products also play a dominant role in the Japanese cooking. Soy sauce, *tofu*, and *miso* are perhaps the best known to the Western world. The fact that the traditional diet consists of a lot of seafood and their own cooking methods has been linked to ''Japanese longevity''.

Japanese cooking was influenced by China in the 8th and 9th centuries, when chopsticks and soy sauce were introduced. In the 13th century, *Zen* Buddhism was introduced also from China. This religion insisted on strict vegetarianism — *Shōjin Ryōri* — *Zen* Temple Cooking, meaning no meat, fish, eggs or dairy products. Before this, meat and poultry were eaten regularly. Japanese culinary tradition had to develop during a long period of isolation from the rest of the world. In the 19th century, Western diplomats brought in their food and their cooking techniques. Thus, Japanese cooking methods as well as eating customs have changed considerably since. But, essentially Japanese cuisine remains what it has been since its earliest times.

Japanese meals are different from those of the West in the way they are served. There are many one-pot dishes cooked at the table. Often the courses are presented all at once and eaten in no particular order. Each dish is served in individual bowls, plates and/or platters for each person. Rice is always served during the courses. In informal way, rice is served with cooked food on top.

Table manners are also different from the Werstern ways. Since everything is eaten with chopsticks, it is good manners to lift the bowl of rice, soup or noodles with the left hand and it is not considered impolite to be a little noisy with soup or noodles. *Sake* (Japanese rice wine) is served with appetizers and more often throughout the meal.

Wine and beer are also popular. *Shōchū*, a sort of mild vodka and *Chū-hai*, its cocktail are also gaining popularity. While *sake* is warmed up and served as a hot drink, *Shōchū* is mixed with lemon juice or other beverages as a cold drink.

Traditionally, desserts are not often served at dinner except for fresh fruit in season followed by hot green tea. The serving portion is small by Western standards, but is arranged so that it may give a sense of visual satisfaction which is partially because meticulous attention is paid to presentation. The mood of the season can be felt in the dishes. Japanese believe all food should be eaten at its best in season.

In general, most of the actual cooking time before serving is rather short because of the preparation beforehand which includes techniques of cutting. For instance, diagonal cutting enlarges the surface to be exposed to the heat cutting down cooking time.

The recipes are given as well as the cutting techniques and cooking methods in detail so that anyone unfamiliar with Japanese cooking can follow and feel confident in achieving good results. Since emphasis has been placed upon the preparation of everyday Japanese meals, no special equipment for any of these dishes is necessary. A reasonably well-equiped Western kitchen will do just as well. However, purchasing some Japanese cooking utensils may be worthwhile and one may find it a pleasure cooking with them (see page 107).

Most of the recipes still retain their authenticity and some are adapted to satisfy "modern tastes". Most of the ingredients are available either in many large supermakets or oriental grocery stores.

There is no need to adhere rigidly to the rules of Japanese cuisine. As you gain proficiency and personal confidence in Japanese cooking, you may like to try *sushi*, *sashimi* or even strict vegetarian cookery (*Zen* Temple Cooking), and go on to *Kaiseki Ryōri* (an offspring of *Shōjin Ryōri*).

The most important thing is to enjoy this whole new sphere of fascinating cooking and to achieve a deep sense of satisfaction.

Tokyo, Japan
February, 1985

Yukiko Moriyama

CONTENTS

BASIC COOKING INFORMATION

★ 1 cup is equivalent to 240 ml in our recipes: (American cup measurement)
      1 American cup = 240 ml = 8 American fl oz
      1 British cup = 200 ml = 7 British fl oz
      1 Japanese cup = 200 ml

1 tablespoon = 15 ml   1 teaspoon = 5ml

C = cup	T = tablespoon	t = teaspoon	fl = fluid	oz = ounce	lb = pound
ml = milliliter	g = gram	in = inch	cm = centimeter	F = Fahrenheit	C = Celsius

TABLES CONVERTING FROM U.S. CUSTOMARY SYSTEM TO METRICS

Liquid Measures

U.S. Customary system	oz	g	ml
1/16 cup = 1 T	1/2 oz	14 g	15 ml
1/4 cup = 4 T	2 oz	60 g	59 ml
1/2 cup = 8 T	4 oz	115 g	118 ml
1 cup = 16 T	8 oz	225 g	236 ml
1 3/4 cups	14 oz	400 g	414 ml
2 cups = 1 pint	16 oz	450 g	473 ml
3 cups	24 oz	685 g	710 ml
4 cups	32 oz	900 g	946 ml

Weights

ounces to grams	
1/4 oz =	7 g
1/2 oz =	14 g
1 oz =	30 g
2 oz =	60 g
4 oz =	115 g
6 oz =	170 g
8 oz =	225 g
16 oz =	450 g

Temperatures

Fahrenheit (F) to Celsius (C)		
freezer storage	−10°F =	−23.3°C
	0°F =	−17.7°C
water freezes	32°F =	0 °C
	68°F =	20 °C
	100°F =	37.7°C
water boils	212°F =	100 °C
	300°F =	148.8°C
	400°F =	204.4°C

Linear Measures

inches to centimeters	
1/2 in =	1.27 cm
1 in =	2.54 cm
2 in =	5.08 cm
4 in =	10.16 cm
5 in =	12.7 cm
10 in =	25.4 cm
15 in =	38.1 cm
20 in =	50.8 cm

Liquid Measures

Japanese system	oz	ml
1/8 cup	7/8 oz	25 ml
1/4 cup	1 3/4 oz	50 ml
1/2 cup	3 1/2 oz	100 ml
1 cup	7 oz	200 ml
1 1/2 cups	10 1/2 oz	300 ml
2 cups	14 oz	400 ml
3 cups	21 oz	600 ml
4 cups	28 oz	800 ml

Deep-Frying Oil Temperatures

300°F − 330°F (150°C − 165°C) = low
340°F − 350°F (170°C − 175°C) = moderate
350°F − 360°F (175°C − 180°C) = high

INGREDIENTS

A.

① DRIED BONITO FLAKES
② *SHIRO MISO*
③ *AKA MISO*
④ *MIRIN*
⑤ RICE VINEGAR
⑥ SESAME OIL
⑦ SOY SAUCE
⑧ LOW−SALT−SOY SAUCE
⑨ LIGHT COLOR SOY SAUCE
⑩ *SAKE*
⑪ PACKED *SAKE*
⑫ HONEY
⑬ CHILI PEPPER OIL
⑭ *SANSHŌ* POWDER
⑮ 7-SPICE POWDER
⑯ DRIED RED PEPPER
⑰ GRATED GINGER IN TUBE

⑱ JAPANESE MUSTARD PASTE IN TUBE
⑲ *WASABI* PASTE IN TUBE
⑳ MUSTARD POWDER
㉑ *DASHI-NO-MOTO* (INSTANT MIX)

① *KOMBU* (KELP)
② DRIED *WAKAME* SEAWEED
③ AGAR-AGAR
④ *NORI* SEAWEED
⑤ CANNED BAMBOO SHOOTS
⑥ CANNED *KAMABOKO*
⑦ *KAMABOKO*
⑧ CANNED *SHIRATAKI*
⑨ RED-VINEGARED GINGER STICKS
⑩ PICKLED PLUM
⑪ GINGER, SWEET-VINEGARED
⑫ DRIED *SHIITAKE* MUSHROOMS
⑬ FREEZE-DRIED *TOFU*
⑭ DRIED CLOUD EAR MUSHROOMS
⑮ DRIED SARDINES
⑯ WHITE SESAME SEEDS

⑰ BLACK SESAME SEEDS
⑱ BEAN THREADS
⑲ RICE VERMICELLI
⑳ DRIED BUCKWHEAT NOODLES
㉑ DRIED THICK WHEAT-FLOUR NOODLES

B.

C.

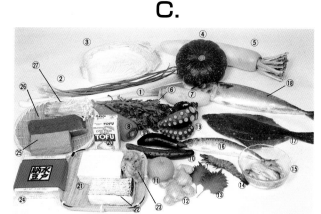

① GREEN ONION
② SCALLION
③ CHINESE CABBAGE
④ JAPANESE PUMPKIN
⑤ *DAIKON* RADISH
⑥ CHRYSANTHEMUM LEAVES
⑦ LOTUS ROOT
⑧ CARROT
⑨ EGGPLANT
⑩ CUCUMBER
⑪ (*YUZU*) CITRON
⑫ FRESH GINGER ROOT
⑬ GREEN *SHISO* LEAVES
⑭ PRAWN
⑮ OYSTERS

⑯ SARDINE
⑰ SOLE
⑱ MACKEREL
⑲ COOKED OCTOPUS TENTACLES
⑳ PACKED *TOFU*
㉑ *TOFU*
㉒ GRILLED *TOFU*
㉓ *GANMODOKI*
㉔ *NATTŌ*
㉕ *ATSUAGE* (DEEP-FRIED *TOFU*)
㉖ *KONNYAKU*
㉗ *ENOKITAKE* MUSHROOMS

FRESH OYSTERS ON THE HALF SHELL *(Namagaki)*

Chilled fresh oysters are a wonderful appetizer.

INGREDIENTS: Makes 8

8 fresh oysters in the shells
***Momiji-Oroshi* (red maple radish)**
⎰ 4 in (10 cm) *daikon* radish
⎱ 3 or 4 dried red chili peppers

* Serve well-chilled half-shell oysters in a bowl of ice with *Momiji-Oroshi* (red maple radish) dip and lemon wedges.
* Shuck oysters. Save liquid for use later. Bed the half-shelled oysters in a bowl of cracked ice and refrigerate while making dip.

1. Peel washed and dried *daikon* radish.

2. Cut stem end of dried red chili peppers and remove seeds.

3. Make 3 or 4 holes in one end of radish with a pointed chopstick.

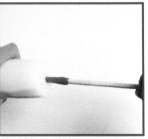

4. Plug seeded and dried red chili peppers into the holes, using the chopstick to push in as shown above. Grate them together so that the radish is flecked with red.

Shiso gives a special flavor to sardines.

INGREDIENTS: Makes 8

4 fresh sardines
8 *shiso* leaves (beefsteak plant; perilla)
$1/2$ stalks celery
4 *shishi-tou* (small green pepper) or 1 medium green pepper, cut into strips
Cornstarch for coating

*See page 98 for selecting and storing fresh fish.

1. Fillet fresh sardines (see page 96); place sardine as shown. Put 2 *shiso* leaves and one *shishitou* on top.

2. Place washed and cleaned julienne strips of celery, 3 or 4 strips each.

3. Roll up toward tail.

4. Secure with toothpick. Dust with cornstarch and deep-fry in 370°F (180°C) oil.

11

GLAZED CHICKEN LIVERS AND GIBLETS *(Motsu no Kushiyaki)*

A simple way to make an ideal snack.

INGREDIENTS: 4 servings

8 oz (225g) chicken livers
8 oz (225g) chicken giblets
Glaze
{ 4 T soy sauce
{ 4 T *mirin*
{ 1 T sugar

1. Wash livers and giblets thoroughly; cut into bite size pieces.

2 Boil the livers and giblets in salted water for 4–5 minutes; drain on a bamboo tray. Skewer 3 pieces of liver or giblet per skewer. Soaking skewers in water prevents burning while grilling.

3. Mix soy sauce, *mirin* and sugar and boil; remove from heat. Brush glaze over skewered livers and giblets several times while grilling, grill about 10 minutes.

STEAMED WONTON (Shūmai)

INGREDIENTS: Makes 22–24

½ lb (225g) wonton skin (24 skins)
10 oz (300g) lean ground beef

A {
  2 T ginger juice or grated fresh
  ginger root
  2 T finely chopped green onion
  1 T soy sauce
  ½ t sugar
  1½ T sesame oil
  2½ T cornstarch
}

2 T green peas

Fried golden brown wontons can be served as hot appetizers.

1. Mix ingredients **A**; add to lean ground beef.

2. Stir and mix well with hands until mixture becomes sticky.

3. Divide into 22–24 fillings or place 2 t filling on center of each wonton skin.

4. Hold wonton skin by finger circle and squeeze into round. Flatten bottom.

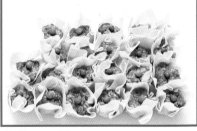

5. Repeat. Place a green pea on center. Coat steamer rack with thin film of oil. Place wontons leaving a small space in between. Steam about 12–14 minutes over high heat.

VARIATION

Place filling on center of each wonton skin. Moisten edges with water; join corners to form triangle. Gather both sides of wonton and press edges to seal. Deep-fry in 360°F (180°C) oil until golden brown.

Fresh red snapper fillets are the tasty key to the success of this soup.

INGREDIENTS: 4 servings

★ Red snapper

7 oz (200g) red snapper fillets
1 green onion
Pinch of salt
Basic Clear Soup Stock
 ⎧ 3 C *dashi* stock (see page 93)
 ⎪ 1t light color soy sauce
 ⎨ ²/₃-1t salt
 ⎩ 1t *sake*

(about 1 cup each)

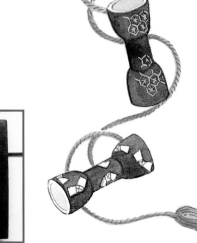

1. Sprinkle red snapper fillets with salt on both sides and let stand for 5 minutes. Rinse in cold water and towel dry; cut into bite size pieces.

2. Heat *dashi* stock; add soy sauce and *sake*. Bring to a boil. Drop red snapper into boiling soup stock and cook for 1 minute. Lift red snapper and place in small soup bowls. Remove scum from soup if any. Pour hot soup into bowls. Garnish with green onion strips and strips of lemon peel.

DIFFERENT COMBINATIONS

A. *Tofu* & *Wakame* seaweed

INGREDIENTS: 1 serving

2/3 C Basic Clear Soup Stock (see page 14)
3 oz (85 g) *tofu*
6 in (15 cm) dried *wakame* seaweed.

Soak *wakame* seaweed in cold water until soft, about 10 minutes. Meantime prepare the Basic Clear Soup Stock. Cut *tofu* in 1/2 in (1.5 cm) cubes. Drain and squeeze *wakame* seaweed; cut away any hard ribs and chop coarsely; place in soup bowl. Heat Basic Clear Soup Stock; add *tofu*. Bring to a boil. Pour into small soup bowl.

B. Chicken & Spinach

INGREDIENTS: 1 serving

2/3 C Basic Clear Soup Stock (see page 14)
1 oz (30 g) skinned and boned chicken breast
1 or 2 spinach leaves

Chop chicken breast and spinach coarsely. Prepare the Basic Soup Stock; add chicken breast. Bring to a boil; remove scum if any. Add spinach and reduce heat; cook just enough to heat spinach through. Pour into small soup bowl.

C. Egg & *Shiitake* mushrooms

INGREDIENTS: 1 serving

2/3 C Basic Clear Soup stock (see page 14)
1 egg
1 small dried *shiitake* mushroom

Soften *shiitake* mushroom (see page 96). Cut into halves. Prepare the Basic Soup Stock. Cook *shiitake* mushroom in soy sauce, sugar, *mirin* over low heat. Break an egg into soup. Cook until egg is poached. Pour into small bowl.

D. Clam & Scallion

INGREDIENTS: 1 serving

2/3 C Basic Clear Soup Stock (see page 14)
2 medium clams
Lemon peel and scallion to garnish, chopped

Soak clam in salted water overnight or at least several hours. Heat Basic Clear Soup stock to a boil; drop in clams. After shells open up, place in a small soup bowl. Strain soup stock. Bring soup stock to a boil; add chopped scallion. Pour into soup bowl. Garnish with strips of lemon peel.

MISO SOUP *(Miso Shiru)*

Miso soup may be served for breakfast, lunch or dinner.

INGREDIENTS: 4 servings

★ *Shijimi* (corbicula clams)

10 oz (300 g) clams or *shijimi* (corbicula clams)
3¹/₃ C *dashi* stock (see page 93)
4 T (80 g) *aka* or *shiro miso*

(about ²/₃ cup each)

1. Soak clams in salted water for 5–6 hours in dark place. Wash and clean. Heat *dashi* stock to a boil; add clams and cook until clams open. Put in small individual soup bowls.

2. Strain soup stock with cheese cloth or paper towel.

3. Mix *miso* and 1 or 2 t *dashi* stock to make paste.

4. Add to *dashi* stock and stir well. Turn off heat right before boiling and pour over clams. Do not overcook *miso* soup as it spoils *miso* aroma.

16

DIFFERENT COMBINATIONS

A. *Tofu* & Scallion

INGREDIENTS: 1 serving

²/₃ C *dashi* stock (see page 93)
1 T (²/₃ oz, 20g) *aka* or *shiro miso*
3 oz (85g) *tofu*
Scallion to garnish

Heat *dashi* stock to a boil; cut *tofu* into ½ in (1.5 cm) cubes and add to the stock. Mix *miso* with some *dashi* stock to make paste; add to the boiling stock. Turn off heat right before boiling. Serve with scallion strips.

B. Potato & Spinach

INGREDIENTS: 1 serving

²/₃ C *dashi* stock (see page 93)
1 T (²/₃ oz, 20g) *aka* or *shiro miso*
½ boiled potato
2 spinach leaves, cooked

Heat *dashi* stock to a boil. Mix *miso* with some *dashi* stock to make paste: add to the boiling stock. Cut potato into small cubes. Chop cooked spinach coarsely. Place potato and spinach in soup bowl. Heat *miso* soup almost to a boil. Turn off heat. Pour into the soup bowl.

C. *Daikon* radish & *Aburage*

INGREDIENTS: 1 serving

²/₃ C *dashi* stock (see page 93)
1 T (²/₃ oz, 20g) *aka* or *shiro miso*
1 *aburage* (deep-fried *tofu* pouch)
¼ C julienne strips *daikon* radish

Put *aburage* into boiling water for a minute to remove excess oil. Cut into julienne strips crosswise. Cook with *daikon* radish in *dashi* stock only for 3–5 minutes. Mix *miso* with some *dashi* stock to make paste: add to the boiling stock, turn off heat; serve.

D. *Wakame* seaweed & Scallion

INGREDIENTS: 1 serving

²/₃ C *dashi* stock (see page 93)
1 T (²/₃ oz, 20g) *aka* or *shiro miso*
4 in (10cm) dried *wakame* seaweed
¼ stalk scallion

Soak *wakame* seaweed until soft. Cut into ¾ in (2cm) pieces; squeeze and place in soup bowl. Chop scallion finely. Bring *dashi* stock to a boil. Mix *miso* with some *dashi* stock to make paste; add to the boiling stock. Bring *miso* soup almost to a boil. Turn off heat. Pour into soup bowl and sprinkle with chopped scallion.

Sashimi

Sashimi is an essential course in any formal dinner in Japan.

INGREDIENTS: 4 servings

7 oz (200 g) *tai* (sea bream)
3½ oz (100 g) *toro* (fattiest tuna)
8 ark shells
5¼ oz (150 g) octopus, cooked
7 oz (200 g) *daikon* radish
½ lemon
Some *kaiware-na* (horseradish sprouts)
Dash of *wasabi*

Sashimi is very fresh fish served au naturel. It is cut into various forms, (flat, cubed, threadlike or paper-thin), and dipped into a mixture of soy sauce and *wasabi* (Japanese green horseradish) and eaten.
* For further details on how to select fresh fish, see page 98.

PREPARATION
* Wipe the surface of sea bream with a wet cloth. Remove "hard scales". Remove head and entrails. Wash thoroughly under running water. Wipe off with a cloth or paper towels. Insert knife under head and slice under-belly as far as backbone. Cut the back in the same way. Cut the meat off from backbone. Cut off small bones along belly. With skin side down, insert knife between skin and flesh in tail end. Pulling end of skin, remove skin carefully. Makes 2 fillets.
* Break one part of ark shell and take the flesh out. Separate the filament and meat. With a knife, scrape off entrails. Wash the meat in salted water to remove sliminess. Pat dry.

1. Slanting knife to the right, cut sea bream and tuna into ¼ in (7 mm) thick slices.

2. Make a few incisions to one end of ark shell.

3. Cut octopus into ¼ in (7 mm) thick slices, moving knife to make ragged surface. Peel *daikon* radish into a continuous paper-thin sheet. Roll and cut into threads; soak in cold water for crispness. Drain well. Arrange with fish on a platter and garnish with *wasabi*, lemon wedges and horseradish sprouts.

BROILED RAINBOW TROUT *(Nijimasu no Shioyaki)*

INGREDIENTS: 4 servings

4 fresh rainbow trout
Salt for coating

*This fish-skewering technique can be applied to any other fresh fish for grilling.

This rainbow trout dish is reminiscence of a scene on the river bank.

1. Scrape off scales. Wipe off surface with a wet cloth. Place fish head to the right. Make a short slit just under fin.

2. Scrape out entrails with care so that shape will be retained.

3. Wash thoroughly under running water. Cut off pectoral fin on both sides.

4. Sprinkle salt on both sides. Place on bamboo tray or rack so that excess water will run off.

5. Hold fish as shown; insert skewer just below eye, under bone, bring the tip out just below the gill flap. Tail will stand erect if skewer is made to come through about 2 in (5cm) from the end of the tail on the same side that the skewer was inserted. The skewer should go in and come out of the same side of the fish.

6. Repeat with one more skewer. Prick skin with a needle to keep shrinkage at a minimum. The skin of very fresh fish shrinks while grilling.

7. Salt tail and fins heavily, as shown. This is "decorative" salting and prevents scorching.

8. Wrap tail and fins with foil. First grill the side that will face up on a plate, until about 60% is cooked. Turn and grill the back side until cooked. Remove skewers by turning gently while fish is hot. Remove the foil after placing on a plate. Garnish with pickled ginger stick or lemon slice if desired.

Fresh ingredients coated with light batter and deep-fried.

INGREDIENTS: 4 servings

12 medium prawns
2 red snapper fillets, or fillets of small white meat fish
2 green peppers
2 Japanese eggplants
2 large dried *shiitake* mushrooms
Tempura Batter
- 2 eggs
- 1½ C iced water
- 2 C sifted all purpose flour

Tempura Dipping Sauce
- 1¾ C *dashi* stock (see page 93)
- ⅓ C soy sauce
- ⅓ C *mirin*

Condiments
Finely chopped scallion
Grated *daikon* radish
Sanshō powder
Salt
Sesame seeds
Lemon juice
Momiji-Oroshi (red maple radish), see page 10

Oil for deep-frying

1. Cut off heads from prawns. Devein and shell as shown with a skewer, leaving tails attached.

2. To prevent prawns from curling while deep-fried, make a few incisions along the belly.

3. To prevent oil splattering while prawns are deep-fried, chop off tips of prawn tails and gently press out water using the side of a knife tip.

4. Cut eggplant lengthwise in halves. Cut off stems. Make deep slits as shown.

5. Cut green peppers lengthwise into quarters and remove seeds. Soak *shiitake* mushrooms until soft. Save soaking liquid for other cooking. Cut mushrooms into quarters.

6. Break eggs into well chilled bowl; add iced water.

7. Add sifted flour.

8. Make lumpy batter. Never mix well. Loosely fold with chopsticks. Batter should be a mixture with lumps of dry flour.

9. Heat oil to 330–355°F (165–180°C) depending on ingredient. Test oil temperature by dropping a tiny bit of batter into the oil; it should float to the surface from halfway to the bottom of the oil. A deep-fry thermometer is useful too.

10. Pat dry or dry all ingredients thoroughly. Begin with vegetables. Coat with lumpy batter; slide into hot oil and deep-fry until golden turning once or twice for even cooking. For prawns pinch tail with fingers; dip into batter, but leaving tail uncoated. Slide into hot oil. Drain excess oil on paper-lined plate or tray after deep-frying.

11. *Tempura* dipping sauce: Bring all ingredients to a boil and let stand to cool.

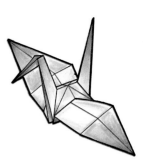

VARIATIONS

★ *TEMPURA* BOWL (*Tendon*)

A combination of shrimp and rice or noodle, is a delicious meal-in-one dish.

INGREDIENTS: 4 servings

5 C cooked rice (see page 90-92)
8 prawn *tempura*
4 *shiitake* mushroom *tempura*
4 green pepper *tempura*
Cooking Sauce
{ 3/4 C *dashi* stock (see page 93)
4 T *mirin*
3-4 T soy sauce
2 t sugar

1. Mix all cooking sauce ingredients; bring to the boil. Add prawns, dried *shiitake* mushrooms, and green peppers *tempura* (2 prawns, 1 mushroom and 1 green pepper per serving) into sauce. Heat them through.

2. In a large bowl put cooked rice; place prawns, mushroom and green pepper *tempura* on top. Pour sauce over and serve.

★ BUCKWHEAT NOODLES WITH *TEMPURA* (*Tempura-Soba*)

INGREDIENTS: 4 servings

9 1/2 oz (275 g) dried buckwheat noodles
8 prawn *tempura*
8 green beans or *shishi-tou* (small green pepper) *tempura*
2 *shiitake* mushrooms *tempura*
Broth for Noodles
{ 5 C *dashi* stock (see page 93)
1/3 C soy sauce
1 T *sake*
1 T sugar
Pinch of salt
Some green onion as garnish

Cook buckwheat noodles as directed on package. Be sure to use large pot so that additional water can be poured in during the cooking. Test the noodle by biting. It should be cooked through to the center, but quite firm. Drain noodles in a colander; rinse off surface starch well under cold running water. Reheat the noodles by plunging into boiling water until hot. Drain and serve in a large noodle bowl. Heat broth in a medium sized pot and bring to a boil. Pour broth over the noodles. Place *tempura* of your choice on top. Garnish with chopped green onion.

21

FISH CAKE AND VEGETABLE CASSEROLE *(Oden)*

This is an attractive dish for a family dinner or for entertaining guests.

INGREDIENTS: 4–6 servings

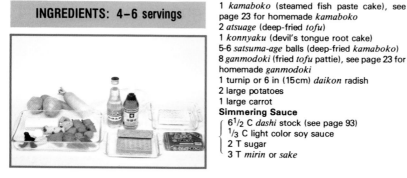

1 *kamaboko* (steamed fish paste cake), see page 23 for homemade *kamaboko*
2 *atsuage* (deep-fried *tofu*)
1 *konnyaku* (devil's tongue root cake)
5-6 *satsuma-age* balls (deep-fried *kamaboko*)
8 *ganmodoki* (fried *tofu* pattie), see page 23 for homemade *ganmodoki*
1 turnip or 6 in (15cm) *daikon* radish
2 large potatoes
1 large carrot
Simmering Sauce
  6$\frac{1}{2}$ C *dashi* stock (see page 93)
  $\frac{1}{3}$ C light color soy sauce
  2 T sugar
  3 T *mirin* or *sake*

Condiments
Mustard
Shichimi tōgarashi (7-spice powder)

PREPARATION
Separate *kamaboko* from the wood, cut crosswise into $\frac{1}{2}$ in (1.5cm) slices. Blanch *atsuage* in boiling water to remove excess oil; cut into quarters or into halves and then diagonally into halves to make triangular shapes. Peel *daikon*, carrot and potato. Cut *daikon* into $\frac{3}{4}$ in (2cm) rounds or half-moons. Cut carrot into $\frac{1}{2}$ in (1.5cm) rounds. Cut potatoes into quarters. Cook all vegetables in boiling water until tender. Save the cooking liquid for other cooking.

1. Rub *konnyaku* with salt; wash and rinse. Cut *konnyaku* into $\frac{3}{4}$ in (2cm) thick pieces. Make an incision in center, about 1 in (2.5cm) long as shown.

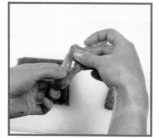

2. Put one end through the cut.

3. Repeat with the rest. Cook in boiling water for 3–4 minutes. Set aside.

4. In a large flameproof earthen-ware pot (*donabe*, see page 111), or slow-cooker, heat *dashi* stock to simmering; add sugar, soy sauce and *mirin*. Add *konnyaku*, *daikon*, carrot, potatoes and *ganmodoki*. Finally add fish products. Simmer over a very low heat for about 1$\frac{1}{2}$ hours.

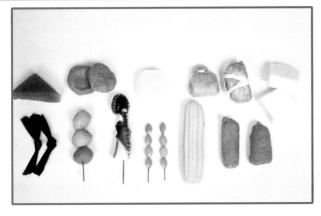

Other suggested ingredients:

Chikuwa (grilled fish paste rolls)
Stuffed *aburage* (thin deep-fried *tofu* pouch)
Kombu (kelp)
Ginkgo nuts
Hard-boiled eggs, shelled
Other fish products as shown
Meat balls
Other vegetables such as squash, pumpkin, kohlrabi
but no red beets

*You can cook with lid or without depending on the type of pot you use. Some fish products should almost float and by the time it is ready to serve, simmering sauce should be reduced by 1/3 at least, so be sure to use enough stock at the beginning. This dish can be served at the table for everyone to help themselves.

VARIATIONS

★ Homemade *Kamaboko*　INGREDIENTS: 2 rolls

18 oz (500g) white fish fillets, skinned
1 egg
1/2 T ginger juice
2–3 T cornstarch

1. Grind white fish meat in an earthen mortar or use food processer. Add egg, ginger juice and cornstarch.

2. Blend well.

3. Divide into halves.

4. Coat aluminum foil with vegetable oil (12 × 10 in, 30 × 25 cm each).

5. Shape *kamaboko* paste like logs about 4 1/2 in (11.5 cm) long. 2 in (5 cm) in diameter. Roll up and seal both ends with aluminum foil.

6. Steam for 30 minutes over high heat. To test the doneness, insert bamboo skewer into center. If skewer comes out clean, it is done. Slice into 1/2 in (1.5 cm) rounds.

★ Homemade *Ganmodoki*　INGREDIENTS: 8 patties

2 1/2 lbs (1125 g) *tofu*, well drained (see page 96)
1 egg white
3 1/2 oz (100 g) carrot
2 dried *shiitake* mushrooms, softened (see page 96)
3T toasted black sesame seeds
A { 1 t *sake*
1 t sugar
1/2 t salt
Small amount of vegetable oil
Oil for deep-frying

1. In food processor, put well-drained *tofu*; puree until smooth at medium high speed. Add **A** and egg white and whip together. Peel carrot and shred finely. Chop softened *shiitake* mushrooms finely. Add carrot, mushrooms, toasted sesame seeds and cornstarch.

2. Blend well at medium high speed for 1 minute. Divide into eights. Make pattie with greased hands. Deep-fry in 335°F (170°C) oil until golden.

23

ASSORTED FISH IN ONE-POT (Yosenabe)

Variety of fish and shellfish eaten with spicy condiments.

3½ oz (100g) *daikon* radish
1¾ oz (50g) carrot
4 dried *shiitake* mushrooms, softened
(see page 96)
½ bunch spinach
2 potatoes
1 leek or 1 bunch green onions
14 oz (400g) Chinese cabbage
7 oz (200g) oysters, shelled
8 large clams
4 shrimps
7 oz (200g) red snapper fillets or firm
fleshed white fish
3½ oz (100g) salmon fillets
12 oz (340g) *tofu*

Simmering Stock
8⅓ C *dashi* stock (see page 93)
3 T light soy sauce
2 T *sake*
3 t salt
Condiments
Scallion, finely chopped
Grated *daikon* radish
Momiji-Oroshi (see page 10)
Lime or lemon juice
Salt
Soy sauce

PREPARATION
Peel *daikon* radish, cut into quarters. Parboil and set aside. Peel carrot, cut into ½ in (1.5 cm) thick rounds (or see page 102); parboil. Cut softened *shiitake* mushrooms into halves. Peel potatoes, cut into chunks; parboil. Cut leek into diagonal slices, cut Chinese cabbage into 1½ in (4 cm) width and spinach into 1⅓ in (3.5 cm) after parboiling. Wash oysters in a colander under cold running water. Clean clams in salted water. Cut off shrimp heads and devein (see page 20). Cut fish fillets into bite size pieces. Cut *tofu* into eight.

DIRECTIONS
Yosenabe is cooked and served at the table in most Japanese homes. When serving at the table, arrange all ingredients attractively on a large platter. You may need more than one platter. Give special attention to color coordination. Prepare a heating unit on a table. Make simmering stock. Fill large *donabe* casserole (see page 111), ⅔ full with simmering stock. Bring stock to a boiling point. Add clams, fish fillets to enrich the stock, then add other ingredients and cook. Add more simmering stock if necessary while cooking. As everyone helps himself, replenish pot with more fresh ingredients.

OYSTER POT (*Kaki no Dotenabe*)

This dish displays oysters simmering in *miso*.

14 oz (400 g) fresh oysters, shelled
1/2 bunch chrysanthemum leaves
1/2 bunch spinach
2 leeks or scallions
1 bunch *enokitake* mushrooms
24 oz (685 g) *tofu*
1-1/2 C water, according to size of pot
Pinch of salt
1 piece 4 in (10 cm) square *kombu* (kelp)
Miso Paste
- 3 1/2 oz (100 g) *aka miso*
- 1 3/4 oz (50 g) *shiro miso*
- 1 1/2 T sugar
- 2 T *mirin*

Condiments
Grated fresh ginger root
Shichimi-tōgarashi (7-spice powder)
Sanshō powder
Lime or lemon

*Since this dish can be served at the table, prepare all ingredients ahead of time and place attractively on a large platter. Cast-iron *suki-yaki* pot, earthen-ware pot or electric skillet can be used as a table-top cooking pot. Have a small serving bowl for each table setting. Season with any of your favorite condiments.

*Slash kelp in a few places so that the flavor will be released.

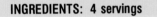

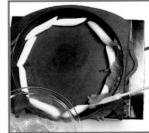

1. Wash oysters in cold water to remove residue and dirt. Sprinkle with some salt while rinsing. Drain and set aside.

2. Cut *tofu* into cubes, cut chrysanthemum leaves and spinach into 2 in (5 cm) length. Cut leeks into diagonal slices and cut off hard stem ends from *enokitake* mushrooms.

3. Mix *miso* paste ingredients; stir well until smooth.

4. Inside the edge of pot, arrange sliced leeks and smooth on a layer of paste. Clean *kombu* (kelp) with damp cloth; place in the center bottom of the pot. Add *tofu* and water; bring to a boil over moderate heat. Lower the heat and add other ingredients for diners. *Miso* paste will dissolve while ingredients are cooked in the pot.

BROILED MACKEREL (Saba no Teriyaki)

Teriyaki sauce gives a lovely taste and texture to broiled mackerel.

INGREDIENTS: 4 servings

1 whole mackerel or 4 mackerel fillets, about 5 1/2 oz (165g) each (*)
Marinade Sauce
- 1/4 C soy sauce
- 1/4 C *mirin*
- 1 T sugar
- 1/2 T grated fresh ginger root

*Yellow tail, tuna, or salmon are also good for broiling.

1. Make an incision at pectoral fin and cut off head. Make a slit in underside of belly.

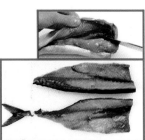

2. Scrape out entrails. Insert the knife into belly, cut along backbone to open out. Cut off tail. Cut the meat off from backbone to make two fillets.

3. Wash and pat dry with paper towel; cut in half. Makes 4 pieces. Mix all marinade sauce ingredients and marinate fish fillets for at least 20 minutes.

4. Broil over charcol fire or in oven. Baste occasionally while broiling. Serve with lemon slice or grated *daikon* radish as a garnish.

SALMON *DENGAKU* *(Sake no Dengaku)*

Miso gives an enchanting flavor to this dish.

4 serving size salmon steaks (＊)
Dengaku Miso Topping
- 2 oz (60 g) *shiro miso*
- 1 T *mirin*
- 1 T *dashi* stock (see page 93)
- 1 egg yolk

＊Red snapper, scallops or other fish fillets can be also used.

1. Broil or bake salmon steaks. In a 2-quart saucepan, mix *miso* topping ingredients except egg yolk and place over hot water. Or put *miso* topping except egg yolk in top of double boiler. Place the top of double boiler over simmering water and stir gently.

2. Add egg yolk and mix thoroughly until smooth and glossy.

3. Baste broiled salmon steaks and broil until topping turns light brown.

STEAMED WHITE FISH (Shiromi-no-Sakana no Mushimono)

This steamed fish is flaky, yet moist inside.

INGREDIENTS: 4 servings

4-5 oz (115-150g) each white meat fish fillets (*)
12-16 oz (340-450g) *tofu*
4 dried *shiitake* mushrooms
1 scallion
4 pieces 2 in (5cm) square *kombu* (kelp)
2 T *sake*
2/3 C *dashi* stock (see page 93)
Condiments
Momiji-Oroshi (see page 10)
Ponzu Sauce (see page 41) or lemon or lime juice with soy sauce

*Flounder, cod, red snapper, sea bass or mackerel.

1. Cut *tofu* into quarters. Soften dried *shiitake* in lukewarm water; cut into halves. In individual heat-proof bowls, place *kombu* on bottom; arrange *tofu*, *shiitake* mushrooms and fish fillets. Pour over 1/2 t *sake* and 1/4 C *dashi* stock. Steam uncovered in hot steamer, for 20 minutes over high heat.

2. Use heat-proof glass ware, 7 × 5 × 1 1/2 in (18 × 13 × 6.5 cm) for steaming 4 pieces of fish fillets. Warm individual bowls in hot water before serving. Garnish with chopped scallion.

SIMMERED SOLE *(Karei no Nitsuke)*

This dish may be served chilled.

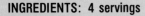

INGREDIENTS: 4 servings

4 fresh sole (∗), about 1/2 lb (225g) each
Simmering Sauce
- 2/3 C *dashi* stock (see page 93)
- 3 T *miso*
- 2 T *sake*
- 2 1/2 T sugar
- 4 T soy sauce

2 green peppers, cut into quarters and seeded
2 T shredded fresh ginger root

∗ Any flat fish (flounder, turbot, halibut and brill) are good.
∗ If fish is large, cut crosswise into appropriate serving sizes.
∗ *Otoshi-buta* (drop-lid, see page 110) is useful for simmering. Aluminum foil, perchment paper or freezer paper cut into circle a little larger than skillet can be a substitute.

1. Scrape off scales using knife; make a short slit in belly on ventral side.

2. Remove entrails carefully with a tip of knife. Wash under running water and wipe dry.

3. Put all simmering ingredients into 12in (30cm) skillet and bring to a boil. Add shredded fresh gingerroot. Put soles in, dorsal side up but do not overlap.

4. Cover with *otoshi-buta*. Simmer 12–13 minutes over low heat, so that the skin of fish does not break off. Arrange the fish on a platter, dark-skin side up and head on left. Cook green peppers in the stock and place on right side.

CHICKEN IN ONE-POT *(Tori no Mizutaki)*

Simmered chicken and vegetables of your choice is a wonderful party dish.

INGREDIENTS: 4–6 servings

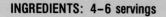

2¹/₂–3 lb (1125–1350 g) chicken
1¹/₄ lb (570 g) Chinese cabbage
1 bunch scallion
12–16 oz (340–450 g) *tofu*
4 in (10 cm) square *kombu* (kelp)
¹/₃ C *sake*
Ponzu Sauce (see page 41)
Condiments
Momiji-Oroshi (see page 10)
Yozu citron or lemon

∗ Whole fryer, thighs, breasts, drum sticks, neck, etc. can be used.

1. Place cut-up chicken in a bamboo tray or colander and pour over boiling water over to remove odor.

2. Cut Chinese cabbage into 2 in (5 cm) widths, cut scallion diagonally and *tofu* into 1 in (2.5 cm) cubes.

3. Wipe *kombu* (kelp) dry with kitchen towel.

4. In a large pot such as an earthenware casserole, place *kombu* (kelp) on bottom and then chicken pieces. Fill the pot with water, cover all chicken pieces and bring to boil.

5. Lift out *kombu* (kelp) and remove scum. Reduce heat; add *sake* and cook for 40 minutes. Add remaining ingredients and simmer until vegetables are tender. Dip into *ponzu* sauce with condiments and eat.

★ QUICK-PICKLED CHINESE CABBAGE (*Hakusai no Ichiya-zuke*)

Cucumbers, turnips, cabbages and other fresh vegetables are excellent for pickling, and the amount can be easily adjusted.

INGREDIENTS

3–3½ lb (1350–1500 g) Chinese cabbage
2 small dried red peppers
4 in (10 cm) square *kombu* (kelp)
1 in (2.5 cm) square fresh ginger root
4 T salt

*For milder and better flavor, sun-dry Chinese cabbage for one day.
*It should be ready to eat on the next day.

1. Cut ⅓ bottom of cabbage into quaters and pull apart by hands. Wash under running water and pat dry.

2. Trim off stem ends of dried red pepper; remove seeds. Cut into ⅛ in (5 m) rounds. Cut *kombu* (kelp) into ¾ in (2 cm) squares, and cut ginger into julienne strips. Mix red pepper, ginger-root, *kombu* (kelp) and salt.

3. Lay cabbage in a large pottery crock, wooden pickle-making tub or plastic tub, cut side out. Sprinkle with salt and kelp mixture. Add another layer, in opposite direction, and sprinkle with salt and kelp mixture; repeat. Cover with drop-lid or wooden board and place some weight on top.

CHICKEN *TERIYAKI* *(Tori no Teriyaki)*

One of the most popular Japanese dishes.

INGREDIENTS: 4 servings

2–3 lb (900–1350g) cut up chicken

Teriyaki Sauce

- 1 T grated fresh ginger root
- 1 clove garlic, crushed
- 2/3 C soy sauce
- 1 T *sake*
- 1/4 C *mirin*
- 3 T sugar

*Shake the skillet to let remaining marinade sauce evaporate. This dish can be served either hot or cold. *Teriyaki* sauce can be used for meat or fish.

1. Wash and clean chicken pieces, towel dry.

2. Make *teriyaki* sauce. Marinate chicken pieces several hours or overnight and keep in refrigerator.

To Bake:
Bake in 325°F (160°C) oven for 45 minutes turning once and baste with marinade sauce.

To Grill:
Place over hot charcoal fire. Brush with marinade sauce when the chicken is half-cooked. Turn several times for even cooking.

To Pan-fry:
Heat about 2 T oil in 12 in (30cm) skillet over medium-high heat; add chicken pieces skin side down and cook until light brown, turn to other side and do the same. Discard grease and add marinade sauce. Cover and reduce heat to low and cook for 6–8 minutes. Remove the lid. Shake the skillet to let remaining marinade sauce evaporate.

STEAMED CHICKEN *(Tori no Mushimono)*

Quick and Easy way to make an elegant dish for calorie cautious people.

INGREDIENTS: 4 servings

1 lb (450 g) chicken breast
2 T *sake*
1 t salt
Condiments
Wasabi and soy sauce
Mayonnaise, lemon juice plus mustard

1. Prick skin with fork to avoid shrinkage while steaming. Sprinkle salt on both sides. Place the chicken skin side up in a heat proof dish and sprinkle with *sake*.

2. Place the dish in a steamer and cover. Steam for 13–15 minutes over high heat; check with bamboo skewer. Insert a skewer in center of meat. It is done when skewer comes out clean. Slice into 3/8 in (1 cm) thicknesses.

DEEP-FRIED ZESTY CHICKEN *(Tori no Tatsuta-age)*

The flavor of fresh ginger turns ordinary chicken into something special.

INGREDIENTS: 4 servings

$1^1/_2$–2 lb (685–900 g) broiler-fryer chicken, cut up
Marinade Sauce
- 4 T soy sauce
- 2 T *sake*
- 1 t ginger juice

Cornstarch for coating
Oil for deep-frying
Condiments
Lemon wedges
Salt and pepper to taste
Soy sauce

∗ For serving with chopsticks, cut chicken into small pieces, or bite size pieces.
∗ For best crispy fried chicken, do not crowd pieces. Keep oil at required temperature. Drain on paper towels.

1. Mix all marinade sauce ingredients. Wash and pat dry cut-up chicken(∗). Marinate chicken for 30 minutes or longer.

2. Drain off excess liquid. Dust chicken pieces with cornstarch.

3. Shake off excess flour. Heat deep-frying oil to 325–350°F (165-175°C). Fry the chicken pieces a few at a time until golden brown.

This is a marvelous dish for lunch.

INGREDIENTS: 4 servings

10½ oz (300 g) skinned and boned chicken breast
4 eggs
4 dried *shiitake* mushrooms
1 onion
Simmering Sauce
  ¼ C water
  4 T soy sauce
  3 T *mirin*
  1 T sugar
5 C cooked rice (see page 90–92)
Mitsuba (trefoil) as garnish, optional

✴ This dish, *Oyako-Donburi*, is a charming culinary expression of ''Parent and Child'' which refers to an omelet on rice made from chicken and egg. The companion dish, *Gyū-don*, with beef and egg omelet on rice is called ''*Tanin-Donburi*''—literal translation; ''Stranger & Child''. (See page 39)

1. Cut the chicken breast diagonally into thin slices. Soak dried *shiitake* mushrooms in lukewarm water until soft. Cut off hard steams and cut into halves. Cut onion into thin slices. Cut *mitsuba* into 1½ in (4 cm) length.

2. In 10 in (25 cm) skillet, mix all simmering sauce ingredients; bring to a boil. Add chicken, mushrooms and onion and cook over moderate heat, 2–3 minutes or until chicken is done and onion is tender.

3. Beat eggs in a small bowl; pour over the chicken and cover with a lid. Cook until the egg is set, about 1 minute over low heat. Sprinkle *mitsuba* on top.

4. To serve, put about 1¼ C cooked rice in a large deep bowl and gently lay ¼ portion of chicken and egg on top of rice. Pour simmering sauce over. Serve immediately or cover with lid.

CHICKEN CURRY RICE

An easy dish using curry mix. Everyone's all time favorite.

INGREDIENTS: 4 servings

1 lb (450g) chicken thigh (＊)
Salt and pepper to taste
2 large onions
2 potatoes
1 carrot
1 box (8½ oz, 240g) instant curry mix(＊)
6 C water
1 clove garlic, optional
2 T oil
5 C cooked rice (see page 90–92)
Condiments
Fukujin-zuke (seven vegetable pickles)
Pickles
Parmesan cheese

＊Beef, pork or shrimp can be substituted for chicken.
＊This Japanese style curry is eaten with spoon in Japan.
＊There are three different types available: mild, medium and hot.

1. Cut chicken thighs into bite size pieces. Sprinkle with salt and pepper. Cut onion into wedges. Peel potatoes and carrots and cut into chunks.

2. Heat 2 T oil in a skillet; sauté chopped garlic, add chicken pieces and stir-fry until light brown; add onions, potatoes and carrots. Stir-fry until onions are tender.

3. Transfer to 3-quart saucepan or to Dutch oven and add 6 C water; cover with a lid. Cook over low heat for 1 hour or until vegetables are done. Remove scum.

4. Turn off heat, add instant curry mix. Return to the stove and stir well over low heat, until thickened. Pour chicken curry over rice.

★ Authentic Chicken Curry

Try an old-fashioned curry when you have time. The spices are most important.

INGREDIENTS: 4–6 servings

1³/₄ lbs (800 g) chicken thighs or cut-up broiler-fryer chicken
Salt and pepper to taste
2 onions
1 tomato
1 instant chicken bouillon cube
2 T vegetable oil
1¹/₂–2¹/₂ C water
16 oz (450 g) plain yogurt

A { 2 T chopped garlic
    1 T julienne strips of fresh ginger

B { 1 t cumin seeds
    ¹/₂ t black pepper
    ¹/₂ t clove
    ¹/₂ t cardamom

C { 5 bay leaves
    ¹/₂ t cumin powder
    ¹/₂ t coriander powder
    1 t chili powder
    ¹/₂ t white pepper

DIRECTIONS

1. Cut chicken into serving size; sprinkle with salt and pepper. Set aside. Chop onions and garlic. Chop tomato coarsely.
2. Heat 2 T oil in Dutch oven and add ingredients **A**, then ingredients **B**. Sauté for 1 minute over high heat. Add chopped onion; sauté until color turns amber.
3. Add chicken and reduce heat to medium low; cover with a lid and cook chicken until half done.
4. Add ingredients **C** and chopped tomato; stir and continue to cook adding 1¹/₂ C water and a bouillon cube. Cook 1 hour over low heat. Add more water if necessary and add yogurt during the simmering process, stirring constantly.
5. Pour the chicken curry in a large serving bowl and serve with cooked rice. Condiments and chutney of your choice may be added.

★ Rice Road

Rice has a long history as far back as 4000–3500 B.C.
Biologically, there are two species. One is called ORYZA SATIVA which is grown in Asian countries and the other is called ORYZA GLABERRIMA which is cultivated in Africa. Both species were cultivated in India in the beginning.
Three different types, long-grain, short-grain and round-grain rice have been developed since. Rice cultivation techniques spread to both East and West. It was 1000 B.C. when short grain rice was first brought into Japan through China and Korea. Later on rice was introduced to Persia (Iran) between 522–485 B.C., then to Greece by Persian soldiers and Indian soldiers. Eventually rice cultivating techniques reached Africa. Since the 7th century, Islamic people seriously started to grow rice as an important food. Today, many areas of the world use rice and each country has developed its own rice recipes. Japanese rice is short-grain which is somewhat stickier and moister than long-grain rice. In the U.S., short-grain rice is grown extensively in California. Newly cropped rice needs less water and slightly shorter cooking time than old rice. Making perfect rice comes with practice. However by adding a pinch of salt with a few drops of vegetable oil to rice or adding other ingredients such as *sake*, perfect rice is easily attainable. See page 90–92 for further details.

★ Curry Powder

Curry powder has long been known to Southeast Asia and Latin America. The bright yellow color and distinctive flavor come from a blend of many spices and herbs. It comes from India, although it is rarely used there. Usually it is made from scratch and each family blends its own according to personal taste. Today, many commercial spice blends are sold at food shops and selecting what kind is a matter of personal taste.

Today *Sukiyaki* is one of the most popular dishes in the world.

INGREDIENTS: 4–6 servings

1 lb (450 g) thinly sliced beef, tenderloin or boneless sirloin (see page 41)
4 leeks, cut diagonally into 2 in (5 cm) pieces
1 onion, cut into wedges
10 oz (285 g) Chinese Cabbage, cut into 1½ in (4 cm) squares
4 oz (100 g) spinach leaves
4 oz (100 g) edible *shungiku* chrysanthemums
2 dried *shiitake* mushrooms, softened (see page 96)
14–16 oz (400–450 g) grilled or regular *tofu*
10 oz (285 g) *shirataki* filaments or bean threads

2–2½ oz (60–70 g) beef suet
Optional Ingredients
Canned bamboo shoots, drained
Canned water chestnuts, drained
Celery stalks
Fresh mushrooms
Carrots, cut diagonally into ⅛ in (5 mm) slices
Green onions
4–6 very fresh eggs
Wari-Shita (Cooking Broth)
⅔ C *dashi* stock (see page 93)
¼ C soy sauce
⅓ C *mirin*
2 T sugar
1 T *sake*

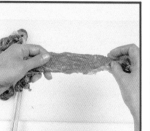

1. Fold thinly sliced wide beef into half lenthwise.

2. Wrap around long cooking chopsticks.

3. Stand chopsticks upright and remove from the meat. This makes a petal.

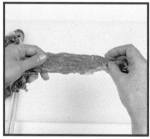

4. Fold thinly sliced beef into half lengthwise.

5. Wrap around the petal. Repeat until you make a large rose-like flower shape.

6. Cut *tofu* into 1 in (2.5 cm) cubes. Parboil *shirataki* filaments; chop roughly. Place all prepared ingredients on a large platter attractively.

7. Heat 12in (3cm) skillet or cast-iron *sukiyaki* pan on heating element to 400°F (205°C) or moderate heat; melt beef suet and grease skillet well.

8. Add a few slices of beef to be cooked.

9. Push to one side and add other ingredients separately; add enough cooking broth to cover 1/3 of ingredients, not too much. Cook more later. Add more broth or water while cooking, adjusting flavor to your taste. Serve with hot *sake* or cold beer if you prefer.

*The authentic Japanese way: Break a fresh egg into a small bowl; dip very hot *Sukiyaki* in it and eat with rice.

★ *Sukiyaki*

The name *Sukiyaki* comes from two words. *Suki* means "hoe" and also means "like, to be fond of" while *Yaki* means "broiled". There are many other theories. Earlier in history, meat-eating was forbidden. Some smart farmers used a hoe as a skillet to cook whatever meat they could find on the spot. For that reason or parhaps not, a shallow cast-iron pan is used for *Sukiyaki*. It is one-pot cookery and is cooked at the table. So much can be prepared ahead of time, and the cooking time itself is short. All ingredients are very attractively assembled on a large platter. Each diner is allowed to choose whatever he or she likes out of simmering flavorful cooking broth. Hot plain rice makes a good accompaniment.

VARIATION

This makes a filling tasty lunch with soup or salad.

★ BEEF BOWL (*Gyūdon*)

INGREDIENTS: 4 servings

5 C cooked rice (see page 90–92)
10½ oz (300g) thinly sliced *sukiyaki* meat (or tenderloin, boneless sirloin), see page 41
4 dried *shiitake* mushrooms, softened (see page 96) and sliced into 1/8 in (5mm)
4 oz (115g) spinach leaves
4 water chestnuts, coarsely chopped
4 eggs
Cooking Sauce
⎰ 1 C water
⎰ ¼ C soy sauce
⎰ ¼ C *mirin*
⎰ 1 t sugar
⎱ 1 T instant *dashi* stock powder

1. In a 12in (30cm) skillet, mix water and instant *dashi* stock powder; cook until dissolved. Add soy sauce, *mirin* and sugar. Add meat; cook for 2–3 minutes.

2. Add *shiitake* mushrooms, water chestnuts and spinach; cook for another 2–3 minutes.

3. Pour beaten eggs over.

4. Cook until eggs are set. Divide into four and place on cooked rice in serving bowl with *sukiyaki* sauce.

Shabu-shabu

Shabu-shabu is eaten with sauce and condiments of your choice.

INGREDIENTS: 4 servings

1 lb (450 g) thinly sliced tenderloin or bone-less sirloin beef, prime-quality well-marbled beef
1¼ lb (600 g) Chinese cabbage
2 leeks or 1 bunch green onion
8 oz (225 g) spinach leaves (8 C)
2⅓ oz (75 g) bean threads or
5 oz (140 g) *shirataki* filaments
4 dried *shiitake* mushrooms, softened (see page 96)
2 quarts (2 liters) *dashi* stock (see page 93) or water

Condiments
Finely chopped green onion
Momiji-Oroshi (see page 10)
Salt and pepper
Soy sauce

DIRECTIONS
1. Fill a heat proof casserole, ⅔ full with *dashi* stock or water; bring to a boil. Start with the meat. Swish back and forth in the broth until meat becomes pink (rare meat is also delicious). Care should be taken not to overcook the meat, as too much heat will toughen it.
2. Each diner may alternate meat and vegetables. The food is dipped in one or another dipping sauce with spicy condiments according to taste. Recipes are provided on next page. Skim off foam occasionally. Add water if necessary.
3. When all the meat, vegetables and noodles are eaten, cooked rice may be added to the broth or you may drink it, lightly seasoned to taste with salt or soy sauce. Stir and ladle the soup into the bowls.

★ *Shabu-shabu*

Shabu-shabu suggests the sound of water simmering stock being swished back and forth by meat which is held by chopsticks. Quality meat is essential, and paper-thin slices take a few seconds to cook. However, an assortment of fresh vegetables takes a little longer. So, cook them according to the "drop-and-retrieve" method. The dipping sauce and spicy condiments listed below provide stimulating contrasts in taste. Each diner can create the flavors he or she desires. As this is a one-pot dish, place a flameproof casserole such as *donabe* (earthenware pot) *sukiyaki-nabe* (cast-iron pan) set on a heating element, or 10–12 in (25–30cm) electric skillet on the table. Since everything is eaten with chopsticks, vegetables are cut into bite-size pieces for cooking. Like other one-pot dishes a lot of the preparation can be done ahead of time. Give meticulous attention to arranging all ingredients in a large, 18 in (45cm) round or oblong platter. Choice of hot *sake*, cold beer or dry red wine goes well with this dish. Serve with hot cooked rice and for dessert, fresh fruit or sherbet with hot green tea to make the perfect meal. Each diner should have chopsticks or a fondue fork. Since there are two dipping sauces, each should have two individual bowls.

The secret of a delicious *Shabu-shabu* is the recipes of sauces.

★ *Ponzu* Sauce

INGREDIENTS: Makes 1 C

1/2 C rice vinegar or
1/2 C lemon juice
1/2 C light color soy sauce

DIRECTIONS
Combine all ingredients well, and stir.

★ Sesame Sauce

INGREDIENTS: Makes 1 C

4 T white sesame seeds
3 T sugar
2 T soy sauce
1 T *shiro miso*
1 T *sake*
3 T *rice* vinegar
1/2 T sesame oil
Shichimi-tōgarashi (7-spice powder)

DIRECTIONS
1. In a dry heavy frying pan, toast sesame seeds over moderate heat, shaking pan for even cooking. As they burn easily, when seeds start to make popping sounds, remove from heat immediately.
2. Grind seeds using a small coffee grinder or *suribachui* (Japanese grinding bowl) See page 111. Ground seeds give a delightful aroma and they should be rough and flaky. Add remaining ingredients to the grinding bowl or transfer the ground seeds to a small bowl. Mix well with a rubber spatula until well blended and smooth.

★ Slicing Meat

Thinly sliced meat is available at Oriental grocery stores or ask your butcher to slice paper-thin. If that is not possible, slice the meat yourself. Freeze meat, about 1 hour. Partially frozen meat can be sliced thinly with a sharp knife. Slice beef against the grain.

BEEF *TERIYAKI* STEAK *(Gyūniku no Teriyaki)*· ROLLED BEEF *(Yawata-maki)*

*"*Teriyaki*" means marinating food in a mixture of soy sauce, *mirin, sake*, fresh ginger or garlic., and glazing on a grill or in a skillet. *Teri* means "glossy shine or glaze" and *yaki* means "broiled or baked".

Yawata-maki

Serve with hot cooked rice if desired.

BEEF *TERIYAKI* STEAK

INGREDIENTS: 4 servings
1 lb ((450g) beef boneless sirloin or tenderloin, cut into 4 steaks
Teriyaki Sauce
- 2 T grated fresh ginger root
- 1/4 C soy sauce
- 1 T *sake*
- 1/2 t sugar
- 1 clove garlic, crushed

Mix all *teriyaki* sauce ingredients; marinate steaks for 1 hour, turning 2–3 times. Cover and refrigerate in hot summer or let stand at room temperature for 30 minutes.

To Grill on a fire:
Start charcoal fire about 1½–2 hours before cooking time. Less intense heat is best for marinated meat while grilling. *Teriyaki* sauce scorches easily. How long, or to what extent meats should be grilled depends on your preference: well-done, medium, rare and so on.

To Pan-broil:
Heat 2 T oil in 12 in (30cm) skillet; brown steaks on one side, covered, over medium high heat for about 3 minutes. Turn over and add reserved marinade sauce; glaze the steaks on both sides, cook 2 to 3 minutes.
Cut steak into 1/2 in (1.5cm) slices, arrange on a plate, and garnish with watercress, grated daikon radish and lemon wedge.

To Broil in an oven:
Set oven control to broil and/or 550°F (290°C). Broil steaks with tops about 4 in (10cm) a part from heat for 5–6 minutes; turn and brush with *teriyaki* sauce; broil another 5–6 minutes.

Yawata-maki

INGREDIENTS: 4 servings
1 lb (450g) thinly-sliced beef sirloin or tenderloin (see page 41)
2 asparagus, steamed
4 green onions
Teriyaki Sauce (see above)
2 T vegetable oil

1. Cut asparagus and green onions into the same length as the width of beef slices. Place on beef as shown.

2. Roll up and secure with a toothpick.

3. Sauté rolled-up beef, shaking the pan for even cooking until light brown. Add *teriyaki* sauce; cover and cook 4–5 minutes over low heat.

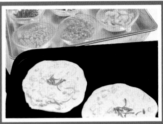

This nutritious lamb and vegetable dish suits a grand party menu.

Teppanyaki

INGREDIENTS: 4–6 servings

1–1$\frac{1}{2}$ lb (450–685g) boneless lamb, thinly sliced or cubed
$\frac{1}{2}$ bunch fresh spinach
8 oz (225g) bean sprouts
2 green peppers (Japanese)
1 onion
2 eggplants
4 dried *shiitake* mushrooms, softened

Okonomiyaki

Oil for grilling

Marinade Sauce
- 1 T garlic, crushed
- 1 T grated fresh ginger
- 3 T white sesame seeds
- $\frac{1}{4}$ C soy sauce
- 2 T vegetable oil
- 1 T sesame oil
- Dash of black pepper

Dipping Sauce
- 3 T *dashi* stock (see page 93)
- 2 T *mirin*
- 3 T soy sauce
- 1 T rice vinegar

Condiments
Finely chopped green onion
Shichimi-tōgarashi (7-spice powder)
Tabasco sauce
Tomato ketchup
Lemon juice

INGREDIENTS: 4 servings

Batter
- $\frac{3}{4}$ C all-purpose flour
- $\frac{1}{3}$ C water
- 1 egg

Fillings
1 C cocktail shrimp, shelled (about 8 oz, 225g)
1 C cabbage, shredded
1 C carrot, finely chopped
1 C canned corn
2 dried *shiitake* mushrooms, softened, hard stems removed, and cut into $\frac{1}{8}$ in (5cm) · wide strips.
$\frac{1}{2}$ C shredded pickled ginger

1. Marinate thinly sliced meat in marinade sauce for 30 minutes.

2. Meantime prepare vegetables; cut green peppers into wedges and remove seeds, cut onion into $\frac{1}{8}$ in (5mm) thick rounds, put a skewer through the center, cut eggplants into half lengthwise. Cut softened *shiitake* mushrooms into halves. Arrange all vegetables attractively on a large platter and meat on another plate. At the table heat electric griddle over high heat (400°F, 205°C); grease lightly. Grill meat and vegetables of your choice, oiling surface frequently. Dip in the sauce with condiments of your choice.

Place each filling into individual dishes. Prepare batter. Heat electric griddle to 400°F (205°C); grease lightly. Pour about 1 T of batter to make 4in (10cm) round pancake. Place fillings of your choice on top; turn over and grill until done. Eat with dipping sauce (see above). Or eat with grated *daikon* radish or mixture of 1t soy sauce and 1t sesame oil. Sprinkle with shredded *nori* seaweed.

PORK CUTLET *(Tonkatsu)*

INGREDIENTS: 4 servings

1 lb (450 g) pork boneless tenderloins or shoulder sliced about $1/2$ in (1.5 cm) thick
2 eggs plus 1 t water
$1/2$ C grated fresh bread crumbs
All-purpose flour for dusting
Vegetable oil for deep-frying
Salt and pepper
***Tonkatsu* Sauce**
{ 4 T Worcestershire sauce
{ 1 T ketchup
Garnishes
Cherry tomatoes
Watercress
Lemon wedge
Condiment
Mustard

Tips for successful deep-frying:
Be sure to check oil temperature by using deep-frying thermometer. Use fresh oil. Remove any scum while deep-frying.

This Japanese version of pork cutlet is most tasty and easy to make.

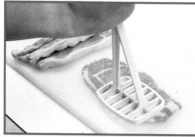

1. Flatten out pork slices.

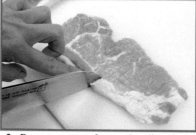

2. Remove excess fat; make slits along fat to prevent shrinkage while cooking. Sprinkle with salt and pepper on both sides; set aside 4–5 minutes.

3. Prepare flour, beaten eggs and bread crumbs in individual containers as shown above. Dust pork fillet with all-purpose flour on both sides, first; shake off excess flour; dip into beaten eggs. Then coat with bread crumbs. Press on both sides.

4. Heat deep-frying oil to 340°F (170°C). Deep-fry pork until done. Pork fillet will sink to bottom at first, then floats on top; turn over 2 or 3 times and cook until golden brown.

5. Drain excess grease on paper towel. Slice and serve.

These pork dishes have long been the most popular items on Japanese restaurant menus.

★ PORK CUTLET ON RICE (*Katsudon*)

INGREDIENTS: 4 servings

4 *tonkatsu* (see left page)
4 C cooked *rice* (see page 90–92)
1 onion, thinly sliced
4 T green peas, cooked
4 eggs
Cooking Sauce
  1²/₃ C *dashi* stock ((see page 93)
  4 t sugar
  5 T soy sauce
  5 T *mirin*

1. Prepare cooking sauce. Divide into four. In a skillet, heat ¼ of cooking sauce and ¼ portion of sliced onion.

2. Add sliced *tonkatsu* (pork cutlet).

3. Pour over 1 beaten egg; cook until egg is set. Sprinkle with 1 T green peas.

4. Serve over hot cooked rice.

★ PORK AND ONION KABOBS (*Kushikatsu*)

INGREDIENTS: Makes 8 kabobs

14 oz (400g) pork (boneless loin), cut into 16 chunks
2 leeks, cut into 1½ in (4cm) lengths
8 *shishi-tou* (small green pepper) or
 4 green peppers; cut into quarters
Salt and pepper
All-purpose flour for dusting
1½–2 C bread crumbs
2 eggs plus 1 t water
Oil for deep-frying
Lemon slices

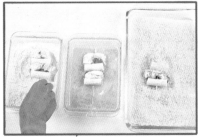

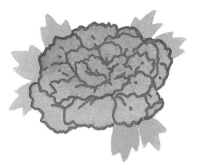

1. Sprinkle pork chunks with salt and pepper. Skewer leeks and pork as shown above. Makes 8 skewers.

2. Coat each skewer with flour, beaten eggs and bread crumbs. Heat oil to 340°F (170°C) and deep-fry 2 or 3 skewers at a time. Turn and cook until golden brown. Drain on paper towel. Deep-fry well-dried green peppers without coating. Put green pepper on top or end of each skewer. Serve with sliced lemon.

GINGER PORK SAUTÉ *(Butaniku no Shōgayaki)*

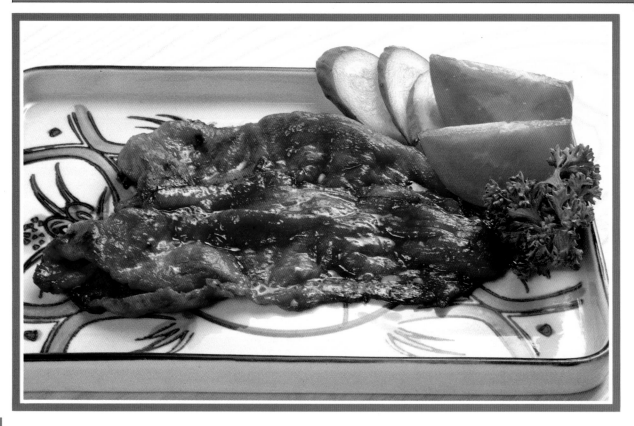

This pork recipe is enhanced with fresh ginger.

INGREDIENTS: 4 servings

14 oz (400g) boneless pork loin, thinly sliced
Marinade Sauce
  1 t ginger juice or 1½ t grated fresh
  ginger root
  4 T soy sauce
  2 T *sake*
  ½ T sugar
3 T oil for grilling
Garnishes
1 cucumber
1 tomato
Parsley

1. Marinate thinly sliced pork loin for 10 minutes. Lift pork slices out and keep marinade sauce.

2. Heat 3 T oil in a 12 in (30cm) skillet over moderate heat; add pork pieces and saute until brown on both sides. As the pork pieces should not overlap each other, cook in batches, adding more oil if necessary.

3. Add reserved marinade sauce; cook the pork over medium high heat, stirring, until the pork is glazed. Arrange the pork on a platter and garnish with tomato wedges and sliced cucumber.

A hearty pork soup is often served as a main dish.

INGREDIENTS: 4 servings

10½ oz (265 g) boneless pork loin, coarsely chopped
2 medium potatoes (about 10½ oz, 265 g)
1 small carrot (approx 3½ oz, 100 g)
4 green onions
7 oz (200 g) *daikon* radish
5–6 T *miso*
1 in (2.5 cm) cube fresh ginger root, chopped
5 C water
1 T oil

*To serve, sprinkle with 7-spice powder or powdered *sanshō*. To save calories, cook pork chunks in water and let stand to cool. Refrigerate overnight. Skim off fat.

1. Cut pork loin into chunks.

2. Cut vegetables into serving size as shown above.

3. In large Dutch oven, heat 1 T oil over high heat; sauté chopped gingerroot and pork chunks; add 5 C water, potatoes, carrot and *daikon* radish. Cook until potatoes are almost done. Add 3 T *miso* and continue to cook until all vegetables are done. Skim scum. Add 3 T *miso* and chopped green onions, stir well. Serve in a large soup bowl.

SAVORY EGG CUSTARD *(Chawan-mushi)*

INGREDIENTS: 4 servings

3 eggs
1²/₃ C *dashi* stock (see page 93)
²/₃ t salt
1 T *mirin*
1 t light color soy sauce
Fillings
3¹/₂ oz (100 g) boned and skinned chicken breast
12 small cocktail shrimp, shelled
4 small dried *shiitake* mushrooms, softened (see page 96)
4 sliced *kamaboko* (steamed fish paste), each ¹/₄ in (7 mm) thick
4 small pieces lime peel

This dish is a light and savory egg custard, an accompaniment for a main dish.

1. Beat eggs. Mix with *dashi* stock and salt. Strain with cloth.

2. Chop chicken breast into small pieces. Add ²/₃ t salt, 1 T *mirin* and 1 t light soy sauce. Slice *shiitake* mushrooms into ¹/₈ in (5 mm) thickness.

3. Place all fillings in bottom of 8 oz (225 g) steaming cups.

4. Stir egg mixture with chopsticks but do not beat. Pour into 4 steaming cups.

5. Break any bubbles on the surface with chopsticks.

6. Place in a hot steamer. Lay kitchen towel between the steamer and lid, and cook over moderate heat 15–20 minutes or until set. Cover and eat with a spoon.

ROLLED OMELET (*Atsuyaki-Tamago*)

INGREDIENTS: Makes 1 roll

6 large eggs
1/3 C *dashi* stock (see page 93)
1/4 t light color soy sauce
2 t *mirin*
1 t sugar
Oil for coating
Condiment
Grated *daikon* radish with soy sauce

[Size: 5 × 2 1/4 × 1 in (13 × 6 × 2.5 cm)]

This is Japanese omelet made from eggs, sweetened with sugar.

1. Mix all ingredients except oil. Heat omelet pan, 5 × 7 × 1 in (13 × 18 × 3 cm), over moderate heat; coat with thin film of oil. Pour small amount of egg mixture to cover the bottom of heated omelet pan.

2. When eggs are almost set, lift one end and fold into three.

3. Push to one end.

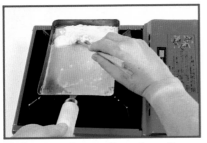

4. Pour another small portion of egg mixture into the pan, lifting cooked egg as shown.

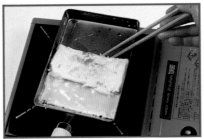

5. Fold into three. Repeat until all egg mixture is used.

6. Place on a bamboo mat and shape like a block of *tofu*. Let stand to cool and slice.

CHILLED *TOFU* JAPANESE STYLE *(Hiya-yakko)*

This is one of the most simple and popular *tofu* dishes.

INGREDIENTS: 1 serving

6 oz (170 g) well chilled tofu, regular or soft
Horseradish sprouts and tomato as garnishes
Condiments
Chopped green onion
Dried bonito flakes
White or black sesame seeds
Grated *daikon* radish
Soy sauce

Chill *tofu* and drain well (see page 96). Place *tofu* in individual bowl and serve with condiments.

★ *Tofu*

Tofu, "bean curd" in English, is an important product of soybeans. It is rich in proteins, vitamins, and minerals. It is low in calories and saturated fats, and entirely free of cholesterol.

There are two main types. One is known as regular *tofu*, and called *momen* (cotton) *tofu*. It is usually called just "*tofu*" as it is used for most dishes.

The other type is called *kinu* (silk) *tofu*. It has a silky smooth texture and delicate flavor. It is most popular in summer as "chilled *tofu*", and is used all the year round for clear soups.

Yaki-dofu (grilled *tofu*) is made of the cotton type *tofu*. It is pressed well before being grilled. It is mainly used in one pot dishes such as *Sukiyaki*.

In this book, "*tofu*" means cotton *tofu*.

Substitute silk *tofu* with cotton *tofu* when you cannot get either as there is little difference in taste.

50

Served as an appetizer or with drinks.

INGREDIENTS: 4 servings

24 oz (720g) regular *tofu* (12 oz, 340g each), well drained (see page 96)
1 T oil
Miso Topping
  2⁴/₅ oz (80g) *shiro miso*
  1 T *mirin*
  1¹/₂ T sugar
  2 T *dashi* stock (see page 93)
  1 egg yolk

1. In a sauce pan, add *miso, mirin*, sugar and *dashi* stock. Cook over low heat stirring constantly until sugar dissolves; add egg yolk and mix well until glossy. Set aside.

2. Cut *tofu* into four crosswise. In a 12 in (30cm) skillet, heat 1 T oil over moderate heat; add tofu and sauté on both sides until light brown.

3. Spread *miso* topping over one side. Skewer each piece with a double-pronged skewer, 3¹/₂ in (9cm) length.

TOFU WITH DRIED BONITO FLAKES (Tosa Tofu)

This lovely combination of *tofu* and dried bonito flakes is a very nutritious appetizer.

INGREDIENTS: 4 servings

14–16 oz (400–460 g) regular *tofu*, well drained
1 egg, beaten
All-purpose flour for dusting
A { 1²/₃ C dried bonito flakes
{ ¹/₃ C black sesame seeds
2 T oil
Garnishes
Chopped green onion
Grated fresh ginger root

1. Cut *tofu* into 1 in (2.5 cm) cubes. Mix **A** and set aside.

2. Coat *tofu* cubes with flour, beaten egg and **A**.

3. In a 12 in (30 cm) skillet, heat 2 T oil over medium high heat; add *tofu* and sauté until brown on both sides. Place on a platter and serve with garnishes mixed with soy sauce.

Okara may be served hot or cold.

1 lb (450g) *okara*

A
- 2 eggs
- ²/₃ C *dashi* stock (see page 93)
- ¼ C light color soy sauce
- 4 T sugar
- 1 t *mirin*

2 T oil

7 oz (200g) frozen mixed vegetables, cooked

Okara looks somewhat like moist sawdust in appearance, but it is highly nutritious soy bean pulp which is a by product of *tofu*. Crumbly and beige-colored okara is fluffy and can absorb any flavor. It contains a fairly high amount of protein. You can obtain it at Oriental food stores or at *tofu* factories.

1. In a large heavy pot, heat 2 T oil over moderate heat; add *okara* stirring constantly and heat through.

2. Add all **A** ingredients and stir well.

3. Add cooked mixed vegetables and toss lightly but well. Serve either hot or cold.

This low in calorie, high in protein dish can be served as a main meal.

INGREDIENTS: 4 servings

4 freeze-dried *tofu*
10¹/₂ oz (300 g) skinned and boned
chicken breast
2 green onions
Simmering Sauce
- 1²/₃ C *dashi* stock (see page 93)
- 2 T sugar
- 3 t soy sauce
- 1 T *mirin*

1. Soak freeze-dried *tofu* in lukewarm water until soft, 2–3 minutes.

2. Squeeze out water and cut into ¹/₂ in (4 cm) lengths. Cut chicken breast into bite size pieces.

3. In a 3-quart saucepan, heat simmering sauce and bring to a boil; add chicken pieces. Bring to a boil again. Skim scum; add *tofu* pieces and reduce heat. Simmer over low heat until liquid is almost absorbed into *tofu*. Add sliced green onion and stir well.

STIR-FRIED DEEP-FRIED *TOFU* *(Atsuage no Itamemono)*

This quick and easy dish can be served with a side serving of rice and soup.

INGREDIENTS: 4 servings

4 *atsuage* (deep-fried *tofu*)
1 lb (450 g) Chinese cabbage
3 T white sesame seeds
Dash of *shichimi-tōgarashi* (7-spice powder)
2 T oil for stir-frying
Cooking Sause

A { 3 T *sake*
  { 5 T soy sauce
  { 1 t *mirin*

1. Mix **A** ingredients; set aside. Dip deep-fried *tofu* into boiling water to remove excess grease; drain. Cut into ¼ in (7 mm) slices crosswise.

2. Wash and clean Chinese cabbage; cut into 1½ in (4 cm) squares.

3. In a wok or 12 in (30 cm) skillet, heat 2 T oil over medium high heat; add cabbage. Stir-fry until cabbage is soft.

4. Add fried *tofu* and mix well. Pour **A** mixture and stir-fry over high heat. Sprinkle with sesame seeds.

TOFU WITH MIXED VEGETABLES *(Tofu no Shira-ae)*

Serve as a side dish with your favorite entrée.

INGREDIENTS: 4 servings

14–16 oz (400–450 g) *tofu*

A
- 1½ T sugar
- Pinch of salt
- ½ T *sake*
- 1 T light color soy sauce

1 cucumber
1 medium carrot
1 *konnyaku* (devil's tongue root jelly), optional

1. In a 2-quart saucepan, boil *tofu* in a generous amount of water for 2–3 minutes. Drain well.

2. Beat cooked *tofu*; add **A** and blend well and smooth.

3. Wash *konnyaku* and slice crosswise into ⅛ in (5 mm) thickness. In Teflon-coated skillet, stir-fry *konnyaku* without any oil for 2–3 minutes. Set aside and let stand to cool.

4. Slice cucumber and carrot thinly into 1½ in (4 cm) long pieces and mix with *tofu*.

56

SIMMERED SOYBEANS *(Daizu no Nimono)*

This low-calorie and low-cost dish is ideal for dinner after a busy day.

INGREDIENTS: 4 servings

1 C dry soybeans
1/2 lb (225 g) drum sticks, or chicken thighs cut into halves
1 in (2.5 cm) square fresh ginger root, thinly sliced
Lemon rind as garnish
3 C water
Simmering Sauce
A { 1/4 C soy sauce
1/4 C *mirin*
1/4 C sugar

1. In a 3-quart saucepan, soak soybeans in water several hours or overnight. Add fresh water to cover the soybeans; cook until soft; drain. Set aside.

2. In a Dutch oven or 3-quart saucepan, pour 3 C water. Wash and pat dry chicken and add to water; add cooked soybeans. Cook over moderate heat; skim scum. Meantime mix **A** ingredients; add to chicken. Add sliced ginger and cook over moderate heat until chicken and soybeans are tender, about 45 minutes. Serve in a bowl garnished with lemon rind.

OCTOPUS SALAD *(Tako-su)* · CRAB MEAT SALAD *(Kani no Sunomono)*

This salad makes a bright and nourishing summer time accompanying dish.

OCTOPUS SALAD

INGREDIENTS: 4 servings

7 oz (200 g) octopus tentacles, cooked
1 cucumber, sliced into thin diagonals
$1/2$ lemon
3 T rice vinegar
Dressing
 { 4 T lemon juice
 { 1 T sugar
 { 3 T soy sauce
Shredded pickled ginger as garnish

1. Slice octopus into $1/8$ in (5 mm) thicknesses. Sprinkle with rice vinegar. Slice lemon.

2. Make dressing. Coat octopus and cucumber slices.

CRAB MEAT SALAD

INGREDIENTS: 4 servings

$5^1/4$ oz (150 g) canned crab meat, drained and cartilage removed
1 lb (450 g) *daikon* radish
$1^3/4$ oz (50 g) carrot
1 lemon as garnish, cut into wedges
Dressing
 { 4 T rice vinegar
 { 1 in (2.5 cm) square fresh ginger root, grated
 { 2 T light color soy sauce

1. Peel outer skin of *daikon* radish and carrot; slice thinly into about $1^1/8$ in (3 cm) length. Soak in water; drain well.

2. Make dressing. Place crab meat, *daikon* radish and carrot in an individual bowl garnished with a lemon wedge. Serve with dressing.

Sesame seeds provide memorable texture and flavor.

CUCUMBER SALAD

INGREDIENTS: 4 servings

1²/₅ oz (40 g) dried *wakame* seaweed
2 cucumbers
¹/₄ C *sanbaizu* (three-flavor vinegar), see page 94
4 t toasted white sesame seeds
A { ²/₃ C water
{ 1 t salt

1. Soak dried *wakame* seaweed in cold water until soft about 20 minutes. Cut away any hard ribs, chop coarsely. Rinse in hot water, then plunge into cold water to retain texture and color. Drain and squeeze.

2. Peel cucumber if waxed. Do not peel Japanese cucumbers. Slice very thinly. Soak in **A** a few minutes; drain and squeeze. Coat *wakame* seaweed and cucumber strips with *sanbaizu* and toss lightly. Serve *wakame* seaweed and cucumber slices in small bowls; sprinkle with toasted sesame seeds.

BEAN SPROUTS SALAD

INGREDIENTS: 4 servings

1 lb (450 g) bean sprouts
10 radishes
Sesame Dressing
{ 2 T *mirin*
{ 5 T rice vinegar
{ 5 T soy sauce
{ 3 T white sesame seeds
Boiling water
1 T rice vinegar

1. Bring water to the boil in a 3-quart saucepan, add 1 T rice vinegar; drop the bean sprouts in cook for 1 minute. Blanch in cold water to retain texture; drain and cool. Slice radishes into thin rounds.

2. Mix bean sprouts and radishes. Just before serving, coat with dressing and toss lightly.

SCALLION SALAD *(Wakegi no Karashi-ae)* · ONION SALAD *(Sarashi Tamanegi)*

These salads may be served as accompaniments for drinks.

SCALLION SALAD

INGREDIENTS: 4 servings

2 bunches scallions
1 lb (450g) *daikon* radish, about 6 in (15cm) long
Mustard Dressing
{ 1 T mustard
{ 2 T soy sauce

1. Fill a 2-quart saucepan with water to ½ full add 2 t salt, bring to the boil; add scallions and cook until tender. Blanch in cold water to retain texture and color; drain and squeeze.

2. Cut into pieces, 1½ in (4cm) long. Peel *daikon* and slice thinly. Mix soy sauce and mustard until smooth. Place scallion and *daikon* in small salad bowls and serve pouring about ½ T dressing on each.

ONION SALAD

INGREDIENTS: 4 servings

2 medium onions
½ C dried bonito flakes
Dressing
{ 1 T vegetable oil
{ 1 T soy sauce
{ 2 T rice vinegar
Salt and pepper to taste

Slice onions into very thin rounds. Soak in cold water, changing water 2–3 times. Drain well. Serve in small salad bowls; sprinkle bonito flakes over. Sprinkle with toasted sesame seeds if desired. Serve with dressing.

STEAMED EGGPLANT SALAD *(Nasu no Mushimono)*

The flavor is enhanced with sesame oil dressing.

INGREDIENTS: 4 servings

6 Japanese eggplants or
4 large eggplants
1 green pepper
1 cherry tomato and parsley as garnishes
Dressing
3 T soy sauce
$\frac{1}{2}$ T sesame oil
1 T rice vinegar
1 T toasted white sesame seeds
1 t *shichimi-tōgarashi* (7-spice powder)
$\frac{1}{2}$ T *mirin*
1 t fresh ginger root, grated

1. Cut eggplants in half lengthwise. Remove stems.

2. With the point of a knife, score each eggplant $\frac{1}{8}$ in (5 mm) deep lengthwise. Each cut should start at just below the stem and extend to the bottom. Steam eggplants for 7 minutes over high heat. Let stand to cool; keep in refrigerator until serving time.

3. Chop green pepper. Arrange chilled eggplants on large platter; sprinkle with chopped green pepper and serve with dressing.

SPINACH SALAD *(Hōrensō no Ohitashi)*

The bright green provides a pleasing color contrast to any dish.

INGREDIENTS: 4 servings

1 bunch spinach(∗), trimmed and washed
Dressing
 {
  ½ C *dashi* stock (see page 93)
  1½ T light color soy sauce
  Pinch of salt
 }
Dried bonito flakes
Nori seaweed for variation

∗ Asparagus and mustard greens are also recommended for this salad.

1. Parboil spinach in lightly salted water until just tender; rinse in cold water to retain color.

2. Place spinach on a bamboo mat and roll up, squeeze out water gently but firmly. This way cooked spinach does not become mushy while being squeezed.

3. Cut off stem ends; cut into 1½ in (4cm) lengths. Place in 4 small bowls. Pour dressing over just before serving and sprinkle bonito flakes on top.

VARIATION
Place *nori* seaweed on a bamboo mat; place cooked spinach as shown and roll up. Slice into 1⅛ in (3cm) thickness. Serve with dressing.

Any green-leaf vegetables go with this dressing.

½ lb (225 g) green beans, washed and trimmed
4 C boiling water
2 t salt
Sesame Dressing
- 4 T black sesame seeds
- 2 T sugar
- 1 T light color soy sauce

★ Sesame Seeds

Both white and black types are available. Black sesame seeds have a slightly stronger flavor and somewhat less oil than the white seeds. Seeds are sold in raw, toasted and ground forms. Keep seeds in an air-tight container and in dry place. Do not buy in large quantity as the oil in sesame seeds gets rancid after some time. Taste seeds before using. If seeds are bitter, throw them away. When using seeds as garnish, use the color that looks the best. It is recommended to use white seeds unless the recipe specifies otherwise. For the best result, toast and grind seeds when needed. The Japanese expression GOMAKASU which is translated as camouflage or to be cheated came from sesame seeds (goma). It is because freshly toasted and ground sesame seeds enhance the overall flavor of any dish and give a delightful aroma.

1. In a saucepan boil 4 C water with 2 t salt, add beans and cook over high heat until done. Rinse beans under cold running water to retain color and crispness. Drain and cut beans into 2 or 3 diagonal pieces. Set aside. In skillet, toast the sesame seeds over moderate heat.

2. Grind seeds using mortar and pestle (see page 111) or a small coffee grinder. Grinding seeds gives delightful aroma. Add sugar and soy sauce and mix well using rubber spatula.

3. Add beans and toss lightly. Serve in 4 small bowls.

SIMMERED CABBAGE AND *SHIITAKE* MUSHROOMS *(Yasai no Fukumeni)*

Cabbage and *shiitake* mushrooms are a wonderful combination.

INGREDIENTS: 4 servings

8 dried *shiitake* mushrooms, softened.
(Reserve soaking liquid)
1/2 head cabbage
Simmering Stock
  1 1/4 C reserved liquid from *shiitake* mushrooms
  1/3 C *mirin*
  3 1/2 T soy sauce

1. Soften *shiitake* mushrooms in luke-warm water until soft. Cut into quarters. Cut cabbage into 1 1/2 in (4 cm) squares.

2. In Dutch oven or large pot, heat simmering sauce over moderate heat to boiling. Add *shiitake* and continue to cook over moderate heat 4–5 minutes.

3. Add cabbage and continue to cook until cabbage is tender.

FLUFFY BOILED POTATOES *(Jagaimo no Tosa-fūmi)*

INGREDIENTS: 4 servings

4 large potatoes
- 3 T light color soy sauce
- **A** ½ t *sake*
- 1 t salt
1 C dried bonito flakes

This light and fluffy potato dish can be served cold or hot to accompany any dish.

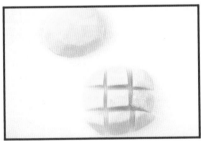

1. Peel potato skins and cut into chunks.

2. Heat water to a boil in a saucepan; add potatoes; reduce heat and cook potatoes until tender. To test, insert bamboo skewer.

3. Discard water; let moisture evaporate by shaking pan over low heat.

4. Mix **A** ingredients; pour into potatoes; toss lightly.

5. Sprinkle dried bonito flakes over the potatoes.

SIMMERED JAPANESE PUMPKIN *(Kabocha no Fukumeni)*

This Japanese version of a pumpkin dish can be served hot or cold.

INGREDIENTS: 4 servings

1¼ lb (600 g) Japanese pumpkin or any winter squash
Simmering Sauce
⅔ C *dashi* stock (see page 93)
¼ C soy sauce
2 T *mirin*
1½ T sugar
Some toasted white sesame seeds

*For microwave oven, cut pumpkin in half and wrap each half in plastic wrap. Turn power level to high and cook 8–10 minutes.

1. Cut pumpkin in half; remove seeds. Cut pumpkin into wedges, 1–1⅛ in (2½–3 cm). Cook pumpkin in a large saucepan covered with water until tender over medium high heat, about 25–30 minutes.

2. Mix simmering sauce ingredients in a saucepan; bring to a boil; add pumpkin wedges. Reduce heat to low and simmer until most of sauce is absorbed into pumpkin. Sprinkle with toasted sesame seeds. For oven method, bake whole pumpkin in 350°F (175°C) oven for 30 minutes or until done.

SIMMERED *DAIKON* RADISH *(Furofuki-Daikon)*

It is simple to make, yet very nutritious and elegant.

INGREDIENTS: 4 servings

18 oz (500 g) *daikon* radish
3 T rice or 2 quarts of rice rinsing water
1 piece of *kombu* (kelp), 2 × 5 in (5 × 13 cm)

Simmering Sauce
- 3–3¹/₃ C *dashi* stock (see page 93)
- 3 T light color soy sauce
- 2 T *mirin*
- 2 T sugar
- 1 t salt

∗ *Daikon* radish holds the heat inside so well that when it is cut with chopsticks steam rises. This is a wonderful winter dish.
∗ Wrap rice with cheese cloth. Water from washed rice gives *daikon* radish a milder taste when cooked.
∗ Clean the *kombu* (kelp) with a damp cloth before adding cooked *daikon*.

1. Cut *daikon* into 1¹/₂ in (4 cm) thick rounds. Peel.

2. Peel a very thin strip from edges of each slice to prevent the *daikon* radish from breaking up while cooking.

3. Make a shallow criss-cross in one side of each slice so that heat can go through.

4. In a saucepan, arrange each slice, cut side down. Cover with water with rice or rice rinsing water and cook until tender; drain. Place cooked *daikon* on the *kombu* (kelp). Fill with simmering sauce and bring to a boil, then reduce heat to low and simmer until soft, about 20 minutes. Arrange *daikon* slices in 4 warmed dishes and pour remaining cooking liquid over.

BAMBOO SHOOTS WITH GROUND PORK *(Takenoko to Hikiniku no Nimono)*

Bamboo shoots play a prominent role in the Japanese kitchen.

INGREDIENTS: 4 servings

18 oz (500 g) canned or boiled bamboo shoots
10½ oz (300 g) ground pork, unseasoned
1 in (2.5 cm) square fresh ginger root, sliced into julienne strips
1 T vegetable oil
Simmering Sauce
  1⅔ C *dashi* stock (see page 93)
  3 T *mirin*
  ¼ C soy sauce
  1 T sugar

1. Cut bamboo shoots in bite size pieces, rolling wedges. Heat 1 T oil in a 12 in (30 cm) skillet over high heat; add ginger and sauté until light brown.

2. Add ground pork and cook over moderate heat until meat turns pink.

3. In a medium saucepan, bring simmering sauce to the boil; add cooked pork.

4. Bring to a boil; skim scum. Add bamboo shoots and simmer over low heat until most of liquid is gone.

The aroma of mild soy sauce stimulates the appetite.

INGREDIENTS: 4 servings

4 ears corn
Glaze
$\left\{\begin{array}{l}\end{array}\right.$ ⅓ C soy sauce
1 T *mirin*

1. Cook corn in lightly salted water until tender.

2. Broil under broiler; turn and brush with glaze.

VEGETABLE *TEMPURA* *(Shōjin-age)*

INGREDIENTS: 4 servings

7 oz (200g) lotus root
4 dried *shiitake* mushrooms, softened
(see page 96)
1 sweet potato
1 potato
1/4 Japanese pumpkin or winter squash
8 strings green beans
8 *shishi-tou* (small green pepper) or
2 green peppers
***Tempura* Batter**
  1 egg
  1 1/4 C iced water
  1 2/3 C all-purpose flour or *tempura*-
  flour
Oil for deep-frying
Condiments
Finely chopped scallion
Grated *daikon* radish
Sanshō powder
Salt
Sesame seeds

1. Peel lotus root, slice into 1/8 in (5mm) thick rounds. Soak in vinegar and water solution, (1T vinegar and 2 C or more water), to prevent discoloration.

2. Cut *shiitake* mushrooms into halves. Slice sweet potato into thin rounds. Peel potato and slice into thin rounds, pumpkin into quarter rounds, green beans into halves and score or prick small green peppers to prevent breaking while being deep-fried.

3. In a chilled bowl, mix egg and iced water.

4. Sift flour and add to egg mixture.

5. Use chopsticks to fold loosely. Batter should not be mixed well. The lumpy batter and powdery ring of flour at sides of the mixing bowl are a good indication.

6. Heat fresh oil in wok or deep-fryer to 340°F (170°C). Pat dry all ingredients with paper towel. Dip thoroughly dried vegetables into batter and deep-fry until golden.

POTATO CROQUETTES

INGREDIENTS: Makes 8–10

1¾–2¼ lb (800–1000 g) potatoes
1 onion, finely chopped
9 oz (250 g) lean ground beef(∗)
1 t salt
Dash of pepper
1 T oil
2 T green peas, cooked
All-purpose flour for dusting, approx 2 C
2 eggs
1½–2 C bread crumbs
Oil for deep-frying
Condiments
Ketchup
Worcestershire sauce
∗ Canned tuna or salmon can be also used.

These nutritious potato croquettes fit perfectly in a grand party menu.

1. Heat 1 T oil; add chopped onion and sauté until transparent. Add ground beef and cook until done, sprinkling on 1 t salt and a dash of pepper. Set aside to cool.

2. Peel potatoes and cut into chunks. Boil potatoes in water until done. Test with bamboo skewer.

3. In a bowl, add potatoes and 1 t salt. Mix and mash. Add cooked green peas.

4. Mix cooled meat and potatoes.

5. Makes 8–10 potato patties.

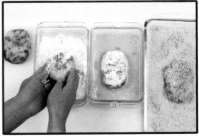

6. Coat the patties with flour, beaten eggs and bread crumbs as shown. Deep-fry in 340–360°F (170–180°C) oil until golden brown.

EDOMAE-SUSHI *(Nigiri-zushi)*

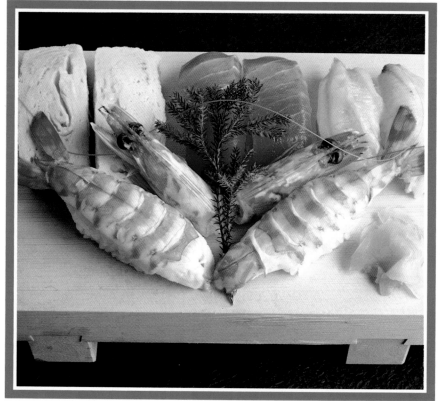

INGREDIENTS: 1 serving

2 large prawns, cooked
2 slices (approx $1/3$ oz, 10g each) geoduck
(horse clam)
2 slices (approx $1/2$ oz, each) fattiest tuna
(*toro*)
2 slices thick omelet (approx $1^2/5$ oz, 40g.)
$2/3$ C prepared *sushi* rice (see page 92)
Other Toppings
Yellow Jack (*Shima-aji*)
Yellowtail (*Hamachi*)
Flounder (*Hirame*)
Gizzard Shad (*Kohada*)
Horse Macherel (*Aji*)
Sardine (*Iwashi*)
Sillago (*Kisu*)
Conger Eel (*Anago*), cooked
Abalone (*Awabi*)
Scallop (*Hotate-gai*)
Ark Shell (*Aka-gai*)
Trough Shell (*Aoyagi*)
Cockle (*Tori-gai*)
Octopus (*Tako*)
Cuttlefish (*Ika*)
Herring Roe (*Kazunoko*), salted

1. Blanch prawns briefly in salted boiling water. Cut off heads and remove shell. Insert knife into belly, and open out. Remove vein along center line using fingers.

2. Blanch geoduck in boiling water 1 minute. Remove the black outer skin and the transparent membrane. Cut diagonally into about $1/3$ oz (10g) slices.

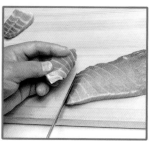

3. Cut tuna diagonally across the lines into $3/8$ in (1 cm) thick slices.

4. Dip both hands into vinegared water (water: vinegar = 3:1). Take some rice (about $2/3$ oz. 20g) in right fingers, hold gently.

5. Take one of toppings in left hand, place a dab of *wasabi* in center with right forefinger. Lay the rice ball on the topping.

6. Holding sides between right thumb and forefinger, roll sushi over so that topping is on top. Press sides with right thumb and forefinger.

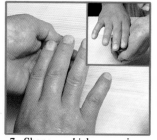

7. Shape *sushi* by pressing top with right fingers, and far end with left thumb.

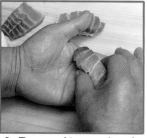

8. Turn *sushi* around and repeat as for 7. Check shape again.

ROLL-YOUR-OWN *SUSHI* (*Temaki-zushi*)

INGREDIENTS: Makes 4 rolls

NATTŌ, SHISO LEAF ROLL
$^2/_3$ C prepared *sushi* rice (see page 92)
2 sheets *nori* seaweed, $8^1/_4 \times 7^1/_4$ in
(21 × 18 cm)
$3^1/_2$ oz (100 g) *nattō* (fermented soy beans)
4 *shiso* leaves
2 T finely chopped green onion
Dash of mustard
Soy sauce

This is an ideal buffet style meal. Let your guests make their own *sushi*.

1. Mix *nattō* with soy sauce and mustard.

2. Cut *nori* seaweed lengthwise into halves.

3. Place *nori* seaweed on left palm, add small amount of rice.

4. Place *shiso*, *nattō* and chopped green onion on top.

★ As occasional substitutes

5. Wrap in nori seaweed.

6. Roll up from left to right.

7. It's ready to eat.

a. Tuna and *Wasabi*

b. Horseradish sprouts, White sesame seeds and *Wasabi*

c. *Takuan* (pickled *daikon* radish) and White sesame seeds

d. Cucumber, Sesame seeds and *Wasabi*

Colorful fillings rolled in *nori* seaweed, cut into thick slices.

LARGE ROLL

INGREDIENTS: Makes 2 rolls

$1^2/_3$ C prepared *sushi* rice (see page 92)
2 sheets *nori* seaweed, $8^1/_4 \times 7^1/_4$ in
$(21 \times 18\,cm)$
$^1/_3$ oz (10g) *kampyō* (dried gourd strips),
see page 78
2 dried *shiitake* mushrooms, cooked (see
page 79)
$^1/_2$ bunch spinach, cooked
1 sheet thin omelet (see page 95)

1 Place *nori* seaweed on bamboo mat, shiny side down; spread half of rice onto *nori* seaweed. Flatten with back of wooden spoon or fingers.

2. Leave $^3/_8$ in (1cm) from front edge and $^3/_4$ in (2cm) from end uncovered.

3. Place all prepared ingredients in center.

4. Lift bamboo mat with thumbs, holding ingredients with other fingers.

5. Roll tightly.

6. Press both ends with fingers.

7. Wet knife and cut in half.

8. Makes 6–8 pieces. Wet knife for each slice to avoid sticking.

SMALL CUCUMBER ROLL

INGREDIENTS: Makes 4 rolls

1²/₃ C prepared *sushi* rice (see page 92)
2 sheets *nori* seaweed, 8¹/₄ × 7¹/₄ in (21 × 18 cm)
1 Japanese cucumber
1 T *wasabi*

1. Cut *nori* seaweed in half lengthwise (4×7 in, 10.5× 18 cm). Place one sheet on a bamboo mat, shiny side down.

2. Cut cucumber into the same length as *nori* seaweed.

3. Cut cucumber in half lengthwise. Cut these pieces again lengthwise to make 4 pieces.

4. Spread ¹/₄ of *sushi* rice onto *nori* seaweed. Leave 1 in (2.5 cm) uncovered at both ends.

5. Put some *wasabi* in center of rice and place a piece of cucumber on top.

6. Start rolling by lifting mat and pressing cucumber with fingers.

7. Roll up tightly. Press ends. Repeat to make 3 more rolls.

8. Put skewers through 4 rolled *sushi* and cut into 4.

INGREDIENTS: Makes 1

2 C prepared *sushi* rice (see page 92)
8 shrimp, cooked and shelled
1/2 cucumber
1 sheet *nori* seaweed, 4 × 7 in (10.5 × 18cm)
1 T black sesame seeds
Dash of *wasabi*

[Size: 8 1/2 × 4 1/4 × 2 1/2 in (22 × 11 × 6cm)]

This is one of the all-time international favorites···shrimp *sushi*.

1. Cut cucumber into 4 in (10cm) length; then slice thinly lengthwise.

2. In a 1.5 liter, 8 1/2 × 4 1/4 × 2 1/2 in (22 × 11 × 6cm) pyrex glass dish, place plastic wrap. Cut cooked shrimp into half lengthwise and place on wrap, skin sides down as shown.

3. Spread 1/2 of *sushi* rice (1 C) and flatten out with spoon.

4. Place sliced cucumbers on rice and sprinkle with sesame seeds.

5. Cover with *nori* seaweed; spread remaining rice on top.

6. Cover with plastic wrap and place some weight on top. Leave for 1 hour. Turn upside-down on a platter and remove the plastic wrap.

PRESSED PICKLED HERRING *SUSHI* *(Nishin no Oshi-zushi)*

INGREDIENTS: Makes 3 bars

3 C prepared *sushi* rice (see page 92)
3 medium herring fillets in vinegar sauce, drained
1/2 Japanese cucumber, thinly sliced
1 T black sesame seeds
Some fresh ginger, sliced into julienne strips

[Size: 7 × 2 × 1 1/8 in (18 × 4.5 × 3 cm)]

The use of pickled herring is characteristic of this *sushi*.

1. Moisten wooden mold. Fill prepared sushi rice half-way up and flatten out.

2. Place thinly sliced cucumber and sprinkle with sesame seeds.

3. Spread rice on top of cucumber slices up to the edges of the mold; flatten with a spoon.

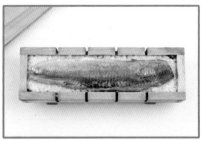

4. Place ginger slices and pickled herring skin side up.

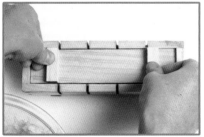

5. Press with wooden lid.

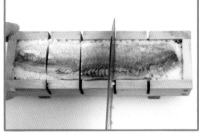

6. Moisten knife and make slits along the wooden mold.

DEEP-FRIED *TOFU* POUCH *SUSHI* (*Inari-zushi*)

INGREDIENTS: Makes 20

3³/₄–4 C prepared *suchi* rice (see page 92)
10 *aburage* (deep-fried *tofu* pouches)

A {
1²/₃ C *dashi* stock (see page 93)
¹/₂ C sugar
3 t *mirin*
4 T soy sauce
}

²/₃ oz (20g) *kampyō* (dried gourd strips)

B {
¹/₃ C *dashi* stock (see page 93)
3 T sugar
3 T soy sauce
}

4 dried *shiitake* mushrooms, softened
(Reserve soaking liquid)
1 small carrot

C {
¹/₃ C *dashi* stock (see page 93)
¹/₃ C *shiitake* soaking liquid
2 T *mirin*
1¹/₂ T soy sauce
1 T *sake*
}

1 Japanese cucumber
Pinch of salt

* Process 10 can be prepared in advance
and frozen for later use.

A Japanese folk tale says this *sushi* is the foxes' favorite.

1. Press *aburage* with rolling pin for easy opening; cut in half.

2. Open *aburage* with thumbs as shown.

3. In a large saucepan, boil 3 C of water. Add *aburage* and cook for 2 minutes to remove excess grease. Drain well.

4. In a large saucepan, heat cooking sauce **A**; add *aburage*. Cook over moderate heat for about 20 minutes or until most of the liquid is absorbed. Allow to cool.

5. Soak *kampyō* (dried gourd strips) in water until soft.

6. Wash in salted water (1 T salt). Rinse well.

7. In medium saucepan, add 2¹/₂ C water. Add *kampyō*; cook 15 minutes; drain.

8. In the saucepan heat cooking sauce **B**; add *kampyō*. Cook over moderate heat for 20 minutes. Allow to cool.

9. Cut into ¼ in (7mm) squares. Set aside.

10. Soften *shiitake* mushrooms; trim stems. Cut into ¼ in (7mm) cubes. Peel carrot; chop finely. Cook mushrooms and carrot in cooking sauce **C**.

11. Slice cucumber finely; soak in salted water. Drain and squeeze well. Mix cooked vegetables with rice; add cucumber. Mix well.

12. Using a spoon fill *abrage* pouches.

VARIATIONS

★ RICE BALLS (*Onigiri*)

★ GRILLED RICE BALLS (*Yaki-Onigiri*)

INGREDIENTS: Makes 12
5 C cooked rice (see page 90–92)
Filling
Cooked or canned salmon, flaked
Canned sardines in tomato sauce, drained and flaked
Takuan (pickled *daikon* radish), chopped
Pickled plums, seeds removed
Dried bonito flakes with soy sauce

Coating
Nori seaweed
Black or white sesame seeds
Pinch of salt
Soy sauce

★ Use wooden mold

1. Moisten wooden mold. Fill mold half full with rice.

2. Press with fitted cover.

3. Make an indentation in center with finger; place fillings of your choice.

4. Cover with rice, press down with the fitted cover. Sprinkle with sesame seeds or wrap with *nori* seaweed.

★ By hand

1. Moisten hands with salty water to prevent sticking. Place a handful of cooked rice (about ½ C) across the bent fingers of the left hand.

2. Make an indentation in center and tuck in one of the fillings.

3. Mold a triangular shape in fingers while pressing onto palm of hands. Sprinkle sesame seeds on both sides or wrap with *nori* seaweed.

★ Grilled rice balls

Brush a bit of soy sauce on grilled rice balls with a touch of melted butter if desired. Ideal for a picnic lunch. Eat with fingers.

OYSTER RICE *(Kaki Gohan)*

INGREDIENTS: 4 servings

2½ C short grain rice
3 C water
1 pint (2 C) small shucked oysters
{ 3 T soy sauce
{ 1 T *sake*
Lemon rinds and *nori* seaweed as garnishes

* If using an automatic rice cooker, wash and rinse oysters and cook with rice from the beginning.

This neatly composed dish can be served as the evening meal.

1. Wash and drain rice.

2. Put oysters in a colander, sprinkling with pinch of salt and wash thoroughly.

3. In a skillet, bring soy sauce and *sake* to a boil and add oysters.

4. Heat through for a minute.

5. Drain oysters and strain the liquid. In a 3-quart saucepan with fitted lid, put rice and 3 C water plus liquid from oysters; cover and cook over moderate heat to boiling.

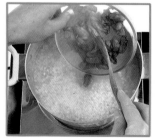

6. Add oysters. Cover and continue to cook for 20 minutes over low heat. Turn off heat and keep covered at least 10 min.

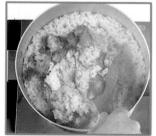

7. Mix rice and oysters lightly.

8. Serve in individual bowls and garnish with shredded *nori* seaweed and lemon rind.

CHICKEN RICE *(Tori Gohan)*

2¹/₂ C short grain rice
3 C water
7 oz (200 g) skinned and boned chicken breast
Marinade Sauce
  1 T soy sauce
  1 T *sake*
  1 t sugar
  1 t grated fresh ginger root
2 dried *shiitake* mushrooms, softened
4 canned water chestnuts
¹/₄ C green peas, cooked

Enchanting chicken and rice dish made quickly and colorfully.

1. Wash and drain rice.

2. Chop water chestnuts finely and slice *shiitake* mushrooms into ¹/₈ in (5 mm) thickness, removing hard stems.

3. Cut chicken breast into bite size pieces and marinate in marinade sauce for 5–10 minutes.

4. In a pot, put rice and water; add fitted lid and cook rice over moderate heat until boiling. Add water chestnuts, mushrooms and drained chicken pieces. Bring to a boil. Cover and cook over low heat for 25 minutes.

5. Turn off heat and let stand for 10 minutes with the lid on. Add cooked peas and toss lightly.

81

This dish is easily digested and quite refreshing for people who have over indulged or are out of sorts.

INGREDIENTS: 4 servings

1 C short grain rice
7 C water
½ bunch Japanese leeks
2 large eggs
A ⎰ ½ T *sake*
⎱ ½ T soy sauce
⎱ ¼ t salt
Condiments
Pickled plums
Shiso leaves
Chinese coriander
Mitsuba (trefoil)
Cooked sardines in tomato sauce
Canned salmon or tuna

Pinch of salt
Soy sauce

* Originally this rice gruel was eaten in *Zen* temples or out of necessity. When an unexpected large number of people visited temples, monks added more water to increase the rice quantity. Today this method of cooking white rice in a lot of water is very popular among Japanese and Chinese. Many different ingredients can be mixed with the rice. The proportions of rice to water; 1:7, 1:10 and 1:15–20.
* Leftover rice can be substituted. Rinse well to get rid of the starch.

1. Bring rice and water to a boil in a large pot or rice cooker over high heat uncovered. Reduce heat to moderate and cook for 30 minutes without stirring. Add ingredients **A**. Mix lightly.

2. Cut leeks into 1 in (2.5 cm) length and add to rice; toss lightly. Cook until leeks are tender and rice is soft and a thick gruel has formed over moderate heat.

3. Add beaten eggs; fold lightly. Cook until eggs are set, remove from the heat and serve immediately. Add some salt if you prefer and add some condiments of your choice; stir and eat with chopsticks or spoon.

CHICKEN NOODLES (Tori no Nikomi Udon)

A favorite on a cold day. This dish is full of tasty ingredients.

INGREDIENTS: 4 servings

10½ oz (300 g) dried thick wheat-flour noodles or
4–7 oz (115–200 g) packages cooked thick wheat-flour noodles
Soup
- 5 C water
- 2½ in (7 cm) square *kombu* (kelp)
- 1½ C dried bonito flakes
- 2 T *mirin*
- 1 T sugar

¼ C light color soy sauce
3½ oz (100 g) skinned and boned chicken breast or lean pork
2 *aburage* (deep-fried *tofu* pouches), see page 78 for oil removal

2 dried *shiitake* mushrooms, softened
4 hard-boiled eggs
½ bunch spinach, cooked
2 green onions
Garnishes
Chopped green onions
Powdered *shanshō*
Pepper

1. Cook noodles as directed on package, adding water while cooking. In a large saucepan, add 5 C water and kelp pieces; cook until water begins to boil. Remove kelp pieces.

2. Add dried bonito flakes in kelp stock and bring to a boil. Turn off heat; strain the stock.

3. Reheat the stock over moderate heat. Add *mirin*, sugar and soy sauce. Add chicken, *aburage* and mushroom pieces to the stock and bring to a boil.

4. Add cooked noodles and cook for 2–3 minutes or longer. Serve in warmed noodle bowls. Place sliced hard-boiled eggs, cut-up spinach on top and garnish with green onions.

CHILLED CHINESE STYLE NOODLES *(Hiyashi Soba)*

INGREDIENTS: 4 servings

10½oz (300g) fresh Chinese-noodles or
4 packages of instant noodles (use
noodles only)
1 Japanese cucumber or
½ regular cucumber, peeled
9 oz (250g) bean sprouts
2 eggs
1 canned crab meat, 5¼ oz (150g),
cartilages removed
Red pickled ginger as garnish
2 t sesame oil
Soup
⎧ 1 C *dashi* stock (see page 93)
⎪ ¼ C sugar
⎨ 6 T rice vinegar
⎪ 6 T soy sauce
⎩ 2 t ginger juice

This is a very refresh-
ing summer dish.

1. In a saucepan, heat soup ingredients until sugar melts over moderate heat. Remove from heat and let stand to cool. Chill until use. Cook noodles; blanch in cold water to remove starch; drain. Sprinkle 2t sesame oil and set aside to cool.

2. Cut cucumber into 2¼ in (6cm) length; then slice thinly.

3. Then, cut into julienne strips.

4. Cook bean sprouts; drain.

5. Make thin egg omelet (see page 95); cut into quarter-rounds.

6. Then, slice thinly as shown above. Place noodles on individual plates, and arrange all ingredients on top and pour chilled soup just before serving. Serve with mustard and chili pepper oil, if desired.

STIR-FRIED RICE VERMICELLI *(Bīfun no Itamemono)*

INGREDIENTS: 4 servings

1½–3 oz (70–85g) rice vermicelli
7 oz (200g) skinned and boned chicken breast

A { ¼ t salt
    { 2 t *sake*

3 green peppers
3 dried *shiitake* mushrooms
2 stalks celery
5¼ oz (150g) cabbage

B { 1 T *sake*
    { 1 t *mirin*
    { 1½t salt

C { ½t sesame oil
    { Dash of pepper

3T vegetable oil

A touch of Chinese flavor adds zest to this dish.

1. Bring a pot of water to a boil and soak rice vermicelli in the boiling water and cook for 2 minutes. Rinse in cold water.

2. Cut the rice vermicelli for easy handling. Drain thoroughly.

3. Marinate chicken pieces in **A**. Trim stems of mushrooms; slice thinly. Cut cabbage into serving size; cut green peppers into quarters lengthwise, remove seeds, and cut celery into diagonal slices.

4. Heat 3T oil in wok or 12in (30cm) skillet; add chicken pieces and sauté until done over high heat.

5. Add vegetables and stir-fry over high heat; add rice vermicelli and ingredients **B** and stir-fry until all vegetables are tender.

6. Add ingredients **C** just before turning heat off. Toss lightly.

SEAWEED PRESERVES *(Tsukudani)*

These are very nutritious dishes using seaweed.

KELP PRESERVES

INGREDIENTS: Makes 1–1¹/₂ C

2 dried *shiitake* mushrooms, softened
(Reserve soaking liquid)
4in (10cm) long *kombu* (kelp) from *dashi* stock
²/₃ C dried bonito flakes or cooked bonito flakes from *dashi* stock

A { 2 T *sake*
1 t rice vinegar
²/₃ C reserved liquid from *shiitake* mushrooms plus water

B { 3–4 T soy sauce
1 T *mirin*

1. Cut *kombu* (kelp) into ³/₄ in (2cm) square pieces, *shiitake* mushrooms into thin slices and mix ingredients **A** together.

2. In a medium saucepan, mix *kombu* (kelp), *shiitake*, and bonito flakes; over medium high heat, bring to a boil. Reduce heat to low and cook 5 minutes; add ingredients **B** and cook until kelp pieces are tender, about 30 minutes.

NORI SEAWEED PRESERVES

INGREDIENTS: Makes ¹/₂ C

10 sheets *nori* seaweed, 12 × 10 ³/₄ in (30 × 27 cm)
1 in (2.5cm) square fresh ginger root, peeled
6 T *sake*
¹/₂ C soy sauce
1 T sugar

DIRECTION

1. Cut *nori* seaweed into 1¹/₂–2in (4–5cm) square pieces. Grate ginger or chop very finely. In medium saucepan, mix all ingredients; cook over medium high heat until boiling. Reduce heat to low and cook until all liquid is absorbed into *nori* seaweed or until mushy, stirring constantly.

* Sometimes unused *nori* seaweed looses its crispness from improper wrapping. This recipe is excellent to rescue the highly nutritious seaweed.

SIMMERED KELP AND LOTUS ROOT *(Kombu to Renkon no Nimono)*

Exotic kelp and lotus root excite the taste buds.

INGREDIENTS: 4 servings

10¹/₂ oz (300 g) lotus root
1 oz (30 g) *kombu* (kelp)
2¹/₂ C water
Simmering Sauce
  { 1¹/₂ T *mirin*
  { 3 T *sake*
  { ¹/₄ C soy sauce

1. Peel lotus root, slice into thin rounds pieces.

2. Soak lotus root in vinegar and water solution to prevent discoloration; rinse and drain.

3. Wipe kelp with damp cloth; cut into ³/₄ in (2 cm) square pieces. In a saucepan, heat 2¹/₂ C water with *kombu* (kelp) and lotus root pieces over moderate heat; cook until tender.

4. Mix *mirin*, *sake* and soy sauce; pour into a pot and cook over moderate heat until most of simmering sauce is absorbed.

These desserts can be conversation pieces as well as tastes.

SNOW WHITE JELLY

INGREDIENTS: Makes 2 cakes
6–8 large strawberries, cut into halves lengthwise
1 bar, 10 × ¼ × 1¼ in (25 × 3 × 3cm) *kanten* (agar-agar) or
2½ T agar-agar powder
1¼ C sugar   2 egg whites
2 C water   1 T lemon juice
[Size: 7½ in (19cm) in diameter and 2½ in (6cm) in hight]

1. Put shredded agar-agar in a saucepan; add 2 C water; set aside about 30 min; bring to a boil, stirring well until agar-agar dissolves. Strain. Reheat the liquid; add sugar and cook until sugar dissolves. Beat egg whites until soft peaks form. Add agar-agar liquid.

2. Continue beating egg whites while adding liquid in a fine stream; add lemon juice and continue to beat mixture for 1 minute longer.

3. Moisten jelly mold with water. Arrange some strawberries in bottom. Spread whipped egg whites adding more strawberries. Set in a pan of cold water or refrigerate until set, about 1 hour.

SWEET POTATOES AND CHESTNUTS

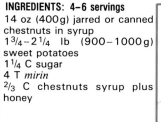

INGREDIENTS: 4–6 servings
14 oz (400g) jarred or canned chestnuts in syrup
1¾–2¼ lb (900–1000g) sweet potatoes
1¼ C sugar
4 T *mirin*
⅔ C chestnuts syrup plus honey

DIRECTIONS
1. Peel sweet potatoes; cook until done; drain. In electric blender or food processor, add all cooked sweet potatoes and beat until smooth.
2. Add sugar, *mirin* and syrup mixture. Beat 1 minute. Transfer sweet potatoes into heavy skillet and cook, stirring constantly over moderate heat, about 10 minutes. Add chestnuts. Mix well.

INFORMATION

PREPARATION

[I] RICE COOKING

★ Types of Rice

There are two main types of rice available; white, short grain Japanese rice, white long grain Chinese rice.

The taste and texture of cooked rice depends on the type and quality of the rice, so you should take great care when selecting it. The best rice to buy for *sushi* is white, short grain Japanese rice.

If you are not familiar with rice, go to a well stocked oriental store and buy a package. If the package is see-through plastic, look for grain that is uniform in size and slightly transparent. Another way to get the best rice is to ask a local *sushi* chef or someone else who would know about Japanese rice.

★ Preparation

Rice increases in volume as it cooks, twice to three times, depending on the kind of rice you use.

If you cook a lot of rice, an automatic Japanese rice cooker will make your work a lot easier, so it's a good investment.

However, a Dutch oven or a pot with a fitted lid and good heat distribution will do just as well.

As a general rule equal amounts of rice and water are sufficient. But short grain rice grown in California may need a little more water ($1/5$ to $1/4$ cup). For regular unseasoned cooked rice, 1 cup of rice with $1\frac{1}{4}$ cups of water will make moist, fluffy rice. Generally cooking 2 cups of rice turns out better than cooking 1 cup.

1. Measure rice carefully.
2. Wash rice in a big bowl of water. Rub grains gently; wet grains break easily.
3. Remove any bran or polishing agent. Drain off water well. Repeat this step three more times or until water is almost clear.
4. Set rice aside for at least 30 min in summer and 1 hour in winter. This allows ample time for rice to absorb the water.
5. In cooking pot, add rice and correct amount of water. Cover with lid.

PREPARATION

★ How to Cook

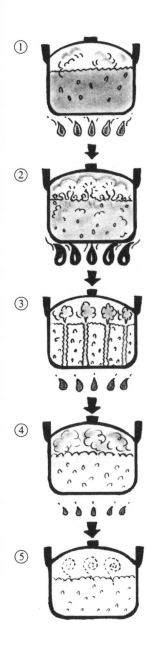

① • MEDIUM HEAT UNTIL WATER BOILS
Cook rice over medium heat until water boils. Do not bring it to boiling point quickly. If the quantity of rice is large, cook rice over high heat from the beginning. The heat can be carried into the center of rice if cooked over medium heat.

② • HIGH HEAT FOR 1 MIN AFTER BOILING
When it begins to   boil, turn heat to high and cook for 1 min. Never lift lid while cooking. Since the lid might bounce from the pressure of the steam, it is better to place a weight, or some dishes on the lid. Rice absorbs enough water.

③ • TURN HEAT TO LOW FOR 4-5 MIN
Turn heat to low and cook for 4-5 min (Be careful not to overboil). Then the pot begins to steam.

④ • THE LOWEST HEAT FOR 10 MIN
Reduce heat to the lowest for 10 min. Every grain of rice absorbs water and becomes plump. It is liable to burn, so cook over the lowest heat.

⑤ • TURN OFF AND LET STAND FOR 10 MIN
Turn off the heat and let rice stand, covered for 10 min. During this 10 min the grains are allowed to "settle", and the cooking process is completed by the heat retained in the rice and the walls of the pot.

• AUTOMATIC RICE COOKER
Today rice is cooked daily in practically every Japanese household in an automatic electric or gas rice cooker. The automatic rice cooker, an appliance developed in the postwar period, cooks perfect rice. Put washed rice in the cooker, add water. There are measurment marks in the cooker for water and rice volume. Then cover and turn on. Automatic controls take over cooking, reducing heat at exact time, and also in some models, the rice is kept warm till needed. Cookers come in various sizes, from tiny ones holding only a few cups to large ones used in restaurants. Automatic rice cookers, either electric or gas can be obtained at oriental stores.

PREPARATION

★ How to Make *Sushi* Rice

*makes softer rice

COOKED RICE	Rice	Water	PREPARED *SUSHI* RICE	VINEGAR MIXTURE		
				Vinegar	Sugar	Salt
2½ C	1 C	1⅕ C	2½ C	2 T	½ T	1 t
5 C	2 C	2 C	5 C	3½ T	1 T	1½ t
7½ C	3 C	*3-3¼ C	7½ C	5 T	1½ T	2 t
10 C	4 C	*4-4½ C	10 C	7 T	2 T	3 t(1T)

C = cup   T = tablespoon   t = teaspoon

The above vinegar mixture proportions are the basic recipe. Sugar can be increased for a sweeter taste.

Prepare a non-metallic tub, preferably a wooden or glass (make sure its not polished since the vinegar will remove the wax polish).

① Wash mixing tub well. Dry with kitchen towel.

② Put cooked rice into mixing tub and spread evenly over the bottom of mixing tub.

③ Sprinkle vinegar mixture generously over the rice. You may not need all of vinegar mixture. Do not add too much liquid.

④ With a large wooden spoon, mix rice with a slicing motion.

⑤ While you mix, use a hand, or an electric fan. This is not to cool *sushi* rice, but to puff the extra liquid away.

⑥ Keep *sushi* rice in the wooden tub, covered with a damp cloth.

PREPARATION

[II] *DASHI* STOCK

The most distinctive thing in Japanese cooking is the use of giant *kombu* (kelp), dried bonito flakes, dried sardines including instant mixes as a basic soup stock. It is said that the first secret of successful Japanese cooking is good *dashi* stock. It is particularly true of clear soup which depends on flavor. So, it is essential to learn how to prepare good basic soup stock. However, instant mixes are readily available–some being excellent. So it may be convenient to have some. Make *dashi* stock according to directions on the package. Leftover *dashi* stock may be stored in the refrigerator for 2–3 days or may be frozen.

★ Makes about 4 C

DASHI STOCK	Water	*Kombu* (Kelp)	Dried bonito flakes	Dried sardines	*Dashi-no-moto* (Instant mix)
Kombu-dashi (Kelp *dashi*)	4 C (1 qt)	1⅓ oz (40 g) or 6 inch (15 cm)			
Katsuobushi-dashi (Dried bonito flake *dashi*)	4 C (1 qt)	1 oz (30 g) or 4 inch (15 cm)	1 C or ⅓–½ oz (10–15 g)		
Niboshi-dashi (Sardine *dashi*)	4 C (1 qt) plus 2T *sake*	1 oz (30 g) or 4 inch (10 cm)		10 dried small sardines	
Instant *dashi*	4 C (1 qt)				⅛ oz (4.5 g) or ⅓ T

• Kelp *dashi* stock:

> Wipe kelp with a damp cloth (do not wash, or much of the flavor will be lost), soak in 4 cups of water, and let sit for an hour. Heat to the boiling point, but remove the kelp just before the water actually boils.

• Dried bonito flake *dashi* stock:

> A) *Ichiban-dashi* (Primary *dashi*): Put kelp in 4 cups of water. Heat, uncovered, over medium high heat until the water reaches boiling point; remove the kelp immediately. Add ¼ cup water and heat. Add 1 cup of dried bonito flakes just before the water reaches boiling point. When the foam begins to rise, reduce heat and simmer for 10 seconds. Turn off heat, and add a pinch of salt which will keep the water from absorbing more bonito flavor and tasting too strong. Let stand until the flakes sink to the bottom. Strain and Store.
>
> B) *Niban-dashi* (Secondary *dashi*): Primary *dashi* is best suited for clear soups. Secondary *dashi* can be used for thick soup, cooking vegetables and many other ways as a cooking stock.
> Place the kelp and bonito flakes reserved from the primary *dashi* in 4 cups water. Heat to the boiling point, reduce heat and simmer for 15 minutes. Turn off heat and strain.

• Sardine *dashi* stock:

> As dried small sardines produce a stock with a strong fish flavor, this stock is used mostly for *miso* soups. Remove head and intestines of 10 pieces of dried sardine. This proccess reduces bitterness and strong fish flavor from stock. After washing, soak in 5 cups of water 2–3 hours. Heat until the water just reaches body temperature. Strain.

• Instant *dashi* stock:

> Add *dashi-no-moto* to boiling water and stir until powder dissolves.
> Variation: Use the liquid in which dried *shiitake* mushrooms have been soaked. Add 1 teaspoon instant mix to 1 cup water and mix with the *shiitake* liquid.

PREPARATION

[III] VINEGAR DRESSINGS

DRESSING	SERVING	Rice vinegar	Soy sauce	Sugar	Salt	*Mirin*	*Dashi* stock
Nihaizu (I) (Two-Flavor Vinegar)	6 T	3 T	1½ T				1½ T
Nihaizu (II) (Two-Flavor Vinegar)	½ C	⅓ C	2 T			2 t	
Sanbaizu (I) (Three-Flavor Vinegar)	6 T	3 T	2-3 drops	2 T	½ t		1½ T
Sanbaizu (II) (Three-Flavor Vinegar)	6 T	⅓ C	½–1 t (Light-color)	1½ T	¼ t		
Amazu (I) (Sweet Vinegar)	5 T	3 T		2 T	¼ t		
Amazu (II) (Sweet Vinegar)	1 C plus 1 T	⅔ C		4 T	1 t		
Ponzu (I) (*Ponzu* Sauce)	6 T	2 T	2 T				2 T
Ponzu (II) (*Ponzu* Sauce)	1¼ C	⅓ C (or lemon juice)	⅓ C				⅓ C
Gomazu (Sesame Vinegar)	1 C	5 T	5 T	White sesame seeds 3 T		2 T	

* See page 93 for *dashi* stock.

The above proportions are for the basic small and large recipes. Sugar can be increased for a sweeter taste. Adjust the amount of sugar to your taste.

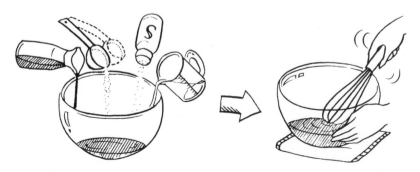

PREPARATION

[IV] *TERIYAKI* SAUCE

INGREDIENT	Soy sauce	Sugar	*Mirin*	*Sake*	Garlic, crushed	Ginger, grated
SEAFOOD (1 lb)	¼ C	1 T	¼ C			½ T
MEAT (1 lb)	¼ C	½ t		1 T	1 clove	2 T
POULTRY (1 lb)	⅔ C	3 T	½ C	1 T	1 clove	1 T

[V] THIN OMELET SHEETS

★ Chicken Eggs

Chicken eggs contain high protein. The protein value is 100 which is the most ideal value of all foods. The white contains pure protein only, but the yolk has iron and vitamin A as well. The yolk also contains lecithin which prevents the increase of cholesterol in the blood. Some analysts report, therefore, that the cholesterol content in the chicken egg is relatively high, but cholesterol in the blood does not increase when they are eaten. The protein content in a chicken egg is about ⅙ oz (5 g) in weight, which is roughly equivalent to that contained in 180cc. of cow's milk. However, it is a representative acid-forming food, therefore you must eat vegetables and/or fruits when eating eggs. To test the freshness of eggs, drop them into water and salt (6%) mixture. Fresh eggs lie on bottom sideways and old eggs will float.

INGREDIENTS

[makes 10-12 sheets]

8 large eggs
2⅔ T cornstarch
2⅔ T water
2 t salt
Oil for frying

[makes 1–2 sheets]

2 large eggs
1 t cornstarch
1 t water
Pinch of salt

[size: 9 in (23cm) in diameter]

① Mix cornstarch, water and salt. Add to beaten eggs.

② Grease teflon coated skillet, 9½ in (24cm) in diameter over medium-low heat. Wipe off excess oil.

③ Pour in just enough beaten egg to cover bottom of skillet.

④ Rotate skillet.

⑤ It's ready when edges curl up and surface becomes glossy.

⑥ Slide out onto waxed paper or plastic wrap. The omelet should be tissue thin. Place paper between each omelet.

PREPARATION

[VI] *SANMAI OROSHI* (Three-part method for filleting fish)

① After soaking in water, remove "hard scales" from tail end. Insert knife under pectral fin at right angles and cut off head.

② Make a slit in belly to anal fin. Remove entrails and wash.

③ Insert knife through back and separate meat along backbone.

④ Two fillets, one with bone.

⑤ Insert knife through the back, work along backbone.

⑥ Remove skeleton.

[VII] DRAINING *TOFU*

As *tofu* holds large amounts of water, sometimes it is necessary to drain or press it well before using.

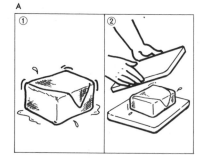

Wrap *tofu* in gauze, place between two boards and let stand to drain.

Boil *tofu* briefly. Wrap in a gauze and place between two boards; let stand to drain.

[VIII] SOAKING DRIED *SHIITAKE* MUSHROOMS

Dried mushrooms must be soaked in warm water until soft, which takes about 1 hour. Place a flat pan lid, drop-lid, or any similar object on mushrooms to keep them submerged. Filling a bowl to the brim with water, adding mushrooms, and laying a plate (that has enough of a curve to keep mushrooms submerged) on top works just as well. Mushrooms soften quicker in warm water than in cold, and a drop-lid not only keeps mushrooms immersed but also prevents water from cooling off, which would slow the softening process. Discard stems and use only caps. Soaking water makes a good stock.

PREPARATION

[VIV] JAPANESE TEAS
★ Green Tea

Green tea is an entrenched part of daily life in Japan.

When guests call, they are always offered tea. Green tea can be served at any time. Green tea is always served immediately after a Japanese meal. Unfermented tea is light and delicate in flavor and is always served plain.

There are two basic types of tea, leaf tea and powdered tea. The powdered tea (*Matcha*) is served only at a formal tea ceremony.

There are a number of grades:

Gyokuro (Best tea)— "jewel dew," the best leaf tea, the first new leaves on the tea bush.

Sencha (Infused tea)—the second best leaf tea.

Bancha (Coarse green tea)— used for everyday tea. In restaurants, *bancha* is always served free of charge.

Tea is brewed in porcelain pots and cups. First, clean and heat the teapot and cups by pouring in brisk boiling water and wait until warmed before discarding the water. Add tea leaves to the warmed pot and pour in fresh hot water. Cover and allow to steep. Then pour into the warmed tea cups. Drain the pot to the last drop.

● *Gyokuro* (Best tea)
<4 servings>
> Warmed small teapot and cups
> 1½ T *Gyokuro* tea leaves
> 2⅔–3 C hot water (about 120°F, 50°C)

> Pour water into the teapot. Let steep for about 1½ minutes. Pour into
> small tea cups.

● *Sencha* (Second-best tea)
> Warmed small teapot and cups
> 2 round t *Sencha* tea leaves
> 1 C hot water (about 170°F, 77°C)

> Pour water into the teapot and let steep for 1 minute. Pour into tea cups.

● *Bancha* (Everyday tea)
> Warmed large teapot and cups
> 3 round T *Bancha* tea leaves
> 3 C boiling water

> Let steep about 2–3 minutes. Pour into tea cups.

★ Other Teas

Hōjicha (Roasted tea)—roasted coarse green tea, for everyday use.

Genmaicha (Rice tea)—mixture of coarse green tea leaves and popped rice.

Mugicha (Barley tea)—roasted barley, a refreshing summer tea served chilled.

Kombucha (Kelp tea)—made from powdered *kombu* (kelp), mild in taste like a light broth.

Sakura-yu (Cherry tea)— Salted cherry blossoms are used for a hot beverage. The cherry tea is customarily served on special occasions—such as betrothals, to honor spring, or welcome the new season.

BASIC COOKING TIPS

★ Soup Making:

Soup plays an important role in a Japanese meal. No Japanese meal is perfect without one soup at least.

There are basically two different kinds of soups, clear and thick soups. Clear soup is usually served at the beginning of a full Japanese meal. Then there is the thick soup. *Miso* soup, fermented soy bean paste soup, is a kind of thick soup. *Miso* soup may be served at the beginning of an informal meal or at the end of a full course meal. It is a must in the traditional Japanese breakfast. Thus millions of Japanese households serve different types of *miso* soup not only at breakfast but at lunch and dinner daily. Japanese clear and thick soups are based on *dashi* stock which differs completely from Western chicken or beef stock. It is based on kelp, dried bonito flakes and dried small sardines. *Dashi* stock is relatively simple to make, but like everything else in the kitchen, it demands attention to detail. See page 93 for basic *dashi* stock recipes.

★ Raw Fish:

Fresh fish that is eaten raw as *sashimi* and *sushi* must be prepared from fish that has not been out of the water for more than 24 hours. Also it must be properly chilled. Otherwise most fish has a shelf life of about five days. Of course the ideal fish is that which you catch yourself.

When buying fish for *sashimi* or *sushi* ask the fishmonger to cut the fish into slices, cubes, whatever you want.

If you are in doubt about the freshness of fish, do not eat it raw. Cook it according to personal preference or marinate it in *teriyaki* sauce and broil. Also no fresh water fish are eaten raw in *sushi* because of the possible presence of parasites. It's similar to eating pork which hasn't been cooked properly. The following are points to check for freshness.

FRESH FISH

1. Mild characteristic odor, but not too strong or "fishy".
2. Bright, full, clear eyes, not milky or sunken.
3. Bright red gills, not muddy gray, free from slime.
4. Bright characteristic sheen on scales.
5. The scales which are adhering tightly to body, unblemished, without any reddish patches along the ventral area.
6. Firm or rigid body when pressed with fingers.
7. Elastic, firm flesh that does not separate easily from the bones or doesn't indent when handled.
8. Freshly cut appearance with no "leathery" traces of yellowing, browning or drying visible in the flesh.
9. Sweetish and often cucumber-like odor.

FROZEN FISH

1. Should be solidly frozen, tightly wrapped with little or no air space between fish and wrapper. Should be moisture vapor-proven.
2. Should be kept at a storage temperature below –10°F (–23°C)in the retail food cabinet.
3. There should be no discoloration, fading or drying out evidence.

STORING FISH

1. Since shellfish and fish are the most perishable foods, they should be used as soon as possible.
2. Wash the fish in cold, slightly salted water. Make sure to wash the cavity well. Remove excess moisture with paper towels. Then wrap in waxed paper or freezer wrap. Keep in the refrigerator. Handle the fish as quickly as possible.

3. Frozen fish should be kept frozen solid in freezer wrap or in a suitable container. Do not thaw frozen fish at room temperature (before cooking), except when necessary for ease in handling. Thawing frozen fish is best achieved at refrigerator temperature. Once the fish has been thawed out, cook it immediately. Never refreeze fish that has been thawed out. It is advisable not to keep fish frozen for more than three months.

To remove the odor from utensils, use solution of baking soda and water. (about 1 tsp. soda to a quart of water).

To get rid of "fishy" odors on the hands or the chopping board, rub with lemon juice, sliced lemon, vinegar or salt before washing and rinse well. A small amount of toothpaste rubbed on the hands and rinsed off is also a good deodorizer.

Wine, vinegar, ginger, lemon, onion, garlic, in the recipe help to minimize the odor of cooked fish.

★ Grilling, Broiling, Pan-frying, Baking:

After eating fish raw, grilling is liked best in Japan. Japan has access to a variety of fish and shellfish in the water surrounding the country. It was natural to eat raw fish and food from the sea has always been valued and appreciated. The Japanese have affection for the sea. When they grill fish, it is served as if the fish on the plate is swimming in the water. The grilling method is used to cook food quickly over very high heat so that the outside is crisp while the inside flesh remains tender and moist. The ingredients must be fresh. Grilling can be done with two different ways; direct heat and indirect. If you do charcoal grill, prepare charcoal fire in advance so that heat gets very hot. For stove top grilling, coat the rack with thin film of oil, then heat unit before you place food on. Fish and meats are often marinated or basted with marinade sauces before and during cooking. Marinade sauces are combinations of *sake, mirin* or sugar, soy sauce and fresh ginger which has the same tenderizing enzyme as papaya and pineapple. Since everything is eaten with chopsticks, food is cut into bite-size pieces except small whole fish. This also reduces both marinating and grilling time. Grill 60% on one side and 40% on the other side. For pan-frying, heat the skillet; add a small amount of oil. Heat the oil, then tilt the skillet to cover the surface of skillet. When the oil begins to form a light haze, it is ready to pan-fry the ingredients. Cook over high heat, so that fish or meat except pork is tender and moist inside and the flavor is sealed in. If longer cooking is necessary, reduce heat and cover for a few minutes. You may need to add some marinade sauce to the pan. Then remove the lid and continue to cook until all liquid evaporates. For oven baking, preheat the oven to the required temperature and place food in the center of the oven to allow for even baking. Microwave oven method is not recommended for Japanese cooking. Microwave cooking takes moisture out of fish and will not give a crispy finish. To eliminate fish odor in the kitchen after cooking, heat a small amount of soy sauce in skillet and burn. The soy sauce aroma helps to remove the fish odor.

BASIC COOKING TIPS

★ Deep-frying:

Tempura is a representative "batter-fried" food in Japan. It is probably the best known Japanese dish.

Four points for successful *Tempura*

1) Fresh ingredients.
2) Good vegetable oil.
3) Constant frying temperature.
4) Lumpy batter.

Prepare all ingredients to be deep-fried ahead of time. Preferably keep in a refrigerator until last minute. Make the *tempura* batter just before the actual deep-frying. The *tempura* batter, mixture of ice water, eggs and flour, should never be stirred well. Mix lightly-batter should be lumpy. All food should be thoroughly dried before dredging. If you prefer a thick coating to thin batter, use less ice water than the recipe (page 20).

In general, deep-frying requires a large amount of oil in the wok, heavy cast iron skillet or deep-fryer. The use of polyunsaturated vegetable oil is strongly recommended for deep-frying. None of the pure vegetable oils contains cholesterol. The right temperature for deep-frying is 330–355°F (165–180°C). The oil should reach this temperature before any ingredients are added. An easy way to tell whether the oil has reached the desired temperature is adding a drop of batter into the oil. If the drop of batter reaches the bottom and slowly returns to the surface, the oil is not yet hot enough. If the batter drops half way to the bottom and immdediately bounces up to the surface, the oil is ready for deep-frying. Drop in ingredients and deep-fry until golden. Adjust the temperature to maintain a constant frying temperature. Frying temperature of 340°F (170°C) is recommended for vegetables. Use deep-frying thermometer to maintain a constant oil temperature. Skim the surface of the oil occasionally to keep it clean. Start with vegetables and then shrimp which requires a higher temperature. The oil used for deep-frying can be saved and reused. To grant your oil longer life, remove crumbs with the fine mesh strainer. The quality of used oil is judged by its clarity, not by the number of times used nor the length of time used. Fresh oil is light in color and clear. If the used oil is still relatively clear, it is readily usable again. For the second time around, it is recommended to deep-fry chicken or meats coated with bread crumbs. To remove odor in oil, deep-fry some potatoes uncoated. The moisture in potato absorbs odor while it is deepfried. The proportion of 3 : 1 (used oil: fresh oil) is also usable again for deep-frying meats and chicken, but not for Tempura. To store the used oil, first strain with a fine mesh strainer while oil is still hot. Then place the oil in a heatproof container and allow to cool. Cover and store in dark and cool place or in the refrigerator.

★ Simmering:

A full course Japanese meal consists of raw fish which is *sashimi*, a broiled or grilled food and a simmered food. So, simmered food plays an important role in the Japanese kitchen.

Simmering food requires special preparation

1) Simmering liquid is generally made of primary *dashi*, *ichiban-dashi* (see page 93) seasoned with *sake*, *mirin* or sugar, salt, soy sauce and/or *miso*. Sake and *mirin* are often used in Japanese cooking. They are mild in taste and add a zest to the food.
2) You may need some special cutting techniques for vegetables such as diagonal slices, flower-cuts, trimming to enhance the appearance of the finished dish.
3) Some ingredients need parboiling to remove harsh or bitter taste and rawness. Also, some ingredients take longer time to cook. These ingredients are sometimes pre-cooked in different pans, then added to the simmering liquid.
   Simmered food can be served as a single dish or as one-pot dish. The ingredients and simmering liquid for the one-pot dishes are prepared ahead of time and arranged attractively on large platters.

The size of the pot is determined by the amount of ingredients to be cooked. For simmering whole fish or fish fillets, use wide flat-bottomed pan. A thick-bottomed pot will do a better job in distributing the heat evenly. If you simmer for longer time, use a deep pot that holds an ample amount of simmering liquid. Electric slow cooker will do the same.
Indispensable when simmering is a drop lid which is a lightweight wooden lid slightly smaller than the pot. It is made of well-dried cypress or cedar. It is placed directly on top of the food to keep them immersed in the liquid, enabling the flavors to be absorbed. Wood is likely to absorb the liquid in the pot and may odors, so always soak the drop-lid in a water for a few minutes before using. Heat-proof flat plate, aluminum foil and heavy butcher-paper are good substitutes for wooden lid. Skim off occasionally. Use light seasoning for simmering liquid. Less is the better. You can always add more later. In general add sugar or *mirin* first, then salt, rice vinegar (if recipe calls for) and soy sauce. Keep in mind to control simmering temperature so that the liquid can be slowly absorbed into the ingredients.

BASIC COOKING TIPS

★ Steaming:

Steaming is one of the best way of retaining more nutrients and natural flavor than other conventional means of cooking. Steaming seals in the natural juices of meats and vegetables which are delicious when served over rice.

There are many different types of steamers available. Wok with a cover will work as a good steamer. Multi-tiered bamboo steamers may be purchased. However, a large pot with a cover will suffice for the purpose of steaming food.

Steaming racks are necessary to support and elevate the plate or bowl which hold food steamed in a wok. A round cake rack will do just as well as commercially available steaming racks. You may improvise, using water chestnut cans with both ends removed. The rack should be put in the center of the wok or pan.

All steamers operate according to the same basic principle. The efficient circulation of steam is of paramount importance. Bamboo steamers have several tiers in which many dishes can be steamed simultaneously. The tiers and cover are set on top of a wok containing boiling water. There are also metal steamers consisting of a pot to hold the water and usually two tiers and a cover. For example, the bottom pot cooks soup stock while the two tiers are used to steam two other separate dishes. In this manner, many dishes may be steamed at a time saving time and energy.

Follow the steps below for effective steaming:

1) Pour water in the wok or pot so that the water level stands one inch below the steaming rack or dish of food.
2) Cover the wok and bring the water to full boil.
3) Use heatproof dishes only for steaming.
4) Place the dish of food atop the steaming rack. Cover and bring to boiling point again. Turn the temperature down to medium high and allow to steam for the specified time.
5) Check the water level when longer steaming is necessary.

★ Stir-frying, Sautéing:

This cooking method combines the elements of high heat and constant tossing to seal in the flavor and juices of meats and vegetables. Thus, this technique is often used for Chinese cooking. Stir-frying cooks protein food thoroughly at the same time leaving it tender and juicy. Vegetables retain their natural color and crisp texture when stir-fried. It is important that slices be uniform in size so that they can be cooked evenly. Some vegetables may need parboiling before stir-frying. Prepare all necessary seasonings before stir-frying. Heat the wok or skillet until it barely gets hot and add a small amount of oil (usually 2 T), then roll the oil around to cover the surface (of the wok). When the oil begins to form a light haze, add the ingredients. Follow the recipe and remember to adjust the temperature control at the proper stir-frying temperature. Actual stir-frying involves vigorous arm action in the constant stirring and tossing of the food. Immediately serve while it is hot.

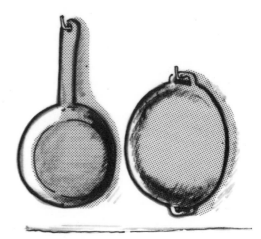

★ Vegetables & Salads:

Many vegetable dishes that would be served hot in Western kitchens are served at room temperature as salads in Japan. The cooking method is to enchance nature's flavor and no matter what a vegetable dish is called, it will be part of a meal with a main course of fish, meat, chicken and so on. Also it can be served as a single dish. Vegetables are washed more often than in the Western kitchen, not only before cooking but also to stop the cooking process and preserve their fresh green color. Also techniques of cutting vegetables are important. Much attention is paid to small details such as assembling vegetables with other food. The portions are small by Western standards. Raw or cooked vegetables are served with dressings. Pour dressing over just before serving.

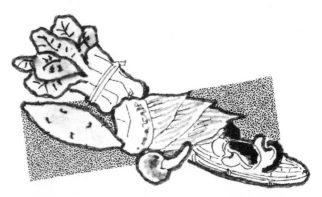

★ Cooking Noodles:

There are varieties of noodles readily available. Packaged noodles made from wheat flour are sold both dried and precooked. Noodle dishes are very popular in Japan and eaten at any time. A hot steaming bowl of noodles in winter and chilled noodle dishes on a hot summer day is refreshing. Cooking noodles is similar to cooking sphaghetti, unless the package has special directions.

Basic cooking method:

Fill ⅔ of a large saucepan with water and bring to a boil. Add the noodles to the boiling water, stirring with chopsticks to keep noodles apart. Bring water to a boil again; add 1 cup of water and bring back to a boil. Repeat the process 2–3 times until noodles are tender. Do not overcook. Drain the noodles in a colander and rinse under cold running water and remove surface starch. Drain. They may be reheated. Put the noodles into a saucepan and pour boiling water over. Let stand for a few minutes, just long enough to heat them through. Drain and serve with dipping sauce or broth. The noodle broth and condiments affect the flavor. Making *dashi* stock is the first step to make good noodle dishes. See page 93 for basic *dashi* stock.

★ Cooking Rice:

Cooking rice translated as "*gohan*" is eaten for breakfast, lunch, dinner, or even in between. Certainly nothing is more important in Japan. Japanese rice is the short-grain kind. There are 200 different varieties of rice growing in Japan. It is almost impossible to try all, but there are a few basic rules to make good cooked rice. Follow the directions on page 91 for regular rice and see page 82 for gruel white rice.

★ Pickling:

Pickles are eaten with many dishes as a garnish to enhance both appearance and taste. There are all sorts of ways to make pickles with different ingredients. But some pickles have an aroma slightly repellent to Westerners—especially rice bran, the most common pickling medium. Pickles do not need to be so strange in taste. Since everyone is very cautious about intake of salt these days, there are many ways to preserve food without heavy salting. Using *kombu* (kelp) is one way. Chinese cabbage, *daikon* radish, cucumber, eggplant and califlower are commonly used for pickling. For quick over-night pickles, see page 31.

CUTTING METHODS

Various cutting methods are introduced in this book. It makes cooking time short, and appearance attractive. For instance diagonal cutting enlarges the surface and it helps the food cook faster. Therefore actual cooking takes only a short time. Since everything is eaten with chopsticks, meat and fish are often cut into bite-size pieces before or after cooking.

[I] BASIC CUTTING METHODS

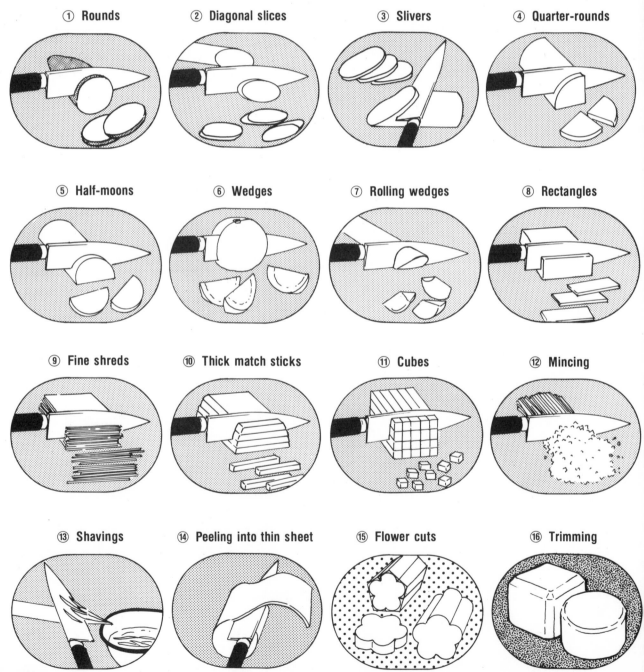

① Rounds　② Diagonal slices　③ Slivers　④ Quarter-rounds

⑤ Half-moons　⑥ Wedges　⑦ Rolling wedges　⑧ Rectangles

⑨ Fine shreds　⑩ Thick match sticks　⑪ Cubes　⑫ Mincing

⑬ Shavings　⑭ Peeling into thin sheet　⑮ Flower cuts　⑯ Trimming

CUTTING METHODS

[II] DECORATIVE CUTTING METHODS

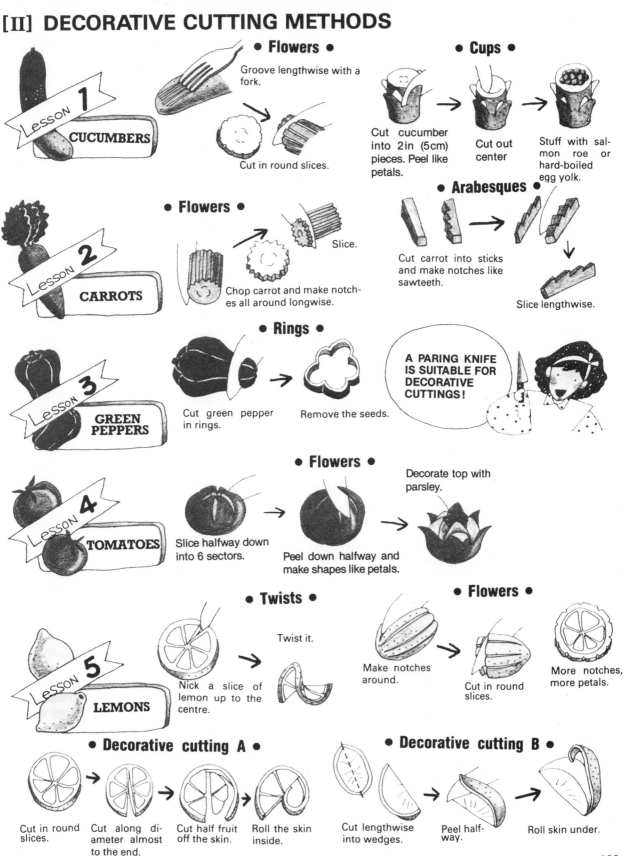

Lesson 1 — CUCUMBERS

• Flowers •
Groove lengthwise with a fork.
Cut in round slices.

• Cups •
Cut cucumber into 2in (5cm) pieces. Peel like petals.
Cut out center
Stuff with salmon roe or hard-boiled egg yolk.

Lesson 2 — CARROTS

• Flowers •
Chop carrot and make notches all around longwise.
Slice.

• Arabesques •
Cut carrot into sticks and make notches like sawteeth.
Slice lengthwise.

Lesson 3 — GREEN PEPPERS

• Rings •
Cut green pepper in rings.
Remove the seeds.

A PARING KNIFE IS SUITABLE FOR DECORATIVE CUTTINGS!

Lesson 4 — TOMATOES

• Flowers •
Slice halfway down into 6 sectors.
Peel down halfway and make shapes like petals.
Decorate top with parsley.

Lesson 5 — LEMONS

• Twists •
Nick a slice of lemon up to the centre.
Twist it.

• Flowers •
Make notches around.
Cut in round slices.
More notches, more petals.

• Decorative cutting A •
Cut in round slices.
Cut along diameter almost to the end.
Cut half fruit off the skin.
Roll the skin inside.

• Decorative cutting B •
Cut lengthwise into wedges.
Peel halfway.
Roll skin under.

103

MENU PLANNING

★ Basic Rules

1. Seasonal appropriateness

Special attention should be given to the ingredients you choose. Some fresh fish and vegetables are available only at certain times of year. Therefore, consider using seasonal ingredients which are abundant in the market.

2. Occasion

To serve a Japanese meal does not have to be so tedious. There are many one-pot dishes cooked at the table.
Consider the number of people you serve and whether you serve for festive occasions, luncheon, dinner, picnic or etc.

3. Flavor and Texture

Plan your menu with meat, fish and vegetables. Make each dish with different cooking method, such as grilled, steamed and fried.

4. Color

Presentation of food is also important. Each ingredient has its different flavor, texture and color. It is important to appeal to the eyes as well as to the tongue.

5. Nutrition

It helps when determining what kind of food to serve to consider the diners' physical conditions and ages.

6. Cost

Seasonal fresh items generally mark lower prices. See the weekly specials for your menu planning.

★ Preparation

[Step I]
1. Read recipes carefully and thoroughly.
2. Write down all necessary ingredients you need to buy.
3. Check all cooking equipment and place within reach.
4. Arrange all necessary seasonings, spices and herbs on kitchen counter or within your reach.
5. Prepare measuring cups and spoons.
6. Prepare all serving bowls, plates and platters near you. You may need to keep some serving platters warm.

[Step II]
1. Put comfortable clothes on and wear an apron, so that you will be psychologically ready for cooking.
2. Prepare plenty of kitchen towels and paper towels.

[Step III]
Hot food should be placed on warmed plate and cold food on chilled plate. Also look at the design on the plate if any before you place food on it. Place the plate so that the design faces the diner. With towel, wipe off around the rim if there are spilled bits or traces of liquid.

MENU PLANNING

★ **Menus for Lunch and Dinner**

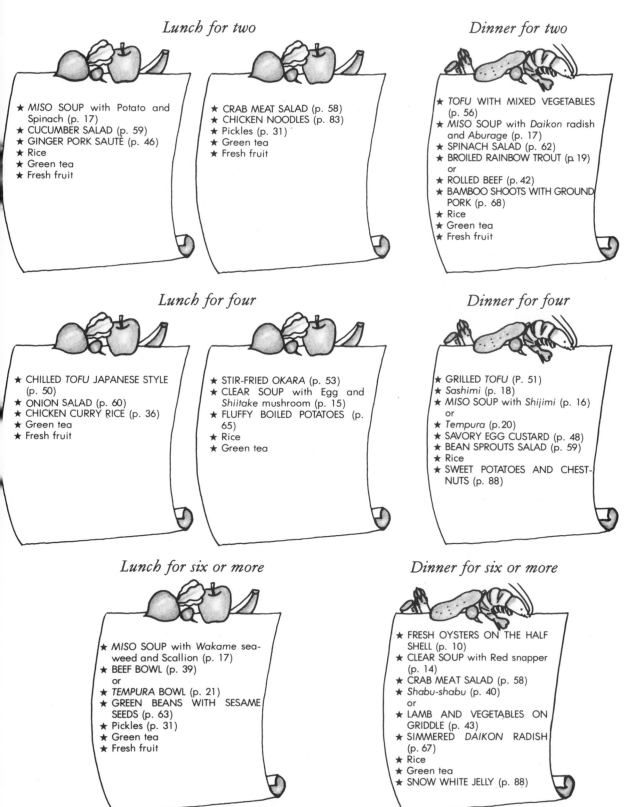

Lunch for two

- ★ *MISO* SOUP with Potato and Spinach (p. 17)
- ★ CUCUMBER SALAD (p. 59)
- ★ GINGER PORK SAUTÉ (p. 46)
- ★ Rice
- ★ Green tea
- ★ Fresh fruit

- ★ CRAB MEAT SALAD (p. 58)
- ★ CHICKEN NOODLES (p. 83)
- ★ Pickles (p. 31)
- ★ Green tea
- ★ Fresh fruit

Dinner for two

- ★ *TOFU* WITH MIXED VEGETABLES (p. 56)
- ★ *MISO* SOUP with *Daikon* radish and *Aburage* (p. 17)
- ★ SPINACH SALAD (p. 62)
- ★ BROILED RAINBOW TROUT (p. 19)
  or
- ★ ROLLED BEEF (p. 42)
- ★ BAMBOO SHOOTS WITH GROUND PORK (p. 68)
- ★ Rice
- ★ Green tea
- ★ Fresh fruit

Lunch for four

- ★ CHILLED *TOFU* JAPANESE STYLE (p. 50)
- ★ ONION SALAD (p. 60)
- ★ CHICKEN CURRY RICE (p. 36)
- ★ Green tea
- ★ Fresh fruit

- ★ STIR-FRIED *OKARA* (p. 53)
- ★ CLEAR SOUP with Egg and *Shiitake* mushroom (p. 15)
- ★ FLUFFY BOILED POTATOES (p. 65)
- ★ Rice
- ★ Green tea

Dinner for four

- ★ GRILLED *TOFU* (P. 51)
- ★ *Sashimi* (p. 18)
- ★ *MISO* SOUP with *Shijimi* (p. 16)
  or
- ★ *Tempura* (p. 20)
- ★ SAVORY EGG CUSTARD (p. 48)
- ★ BEAN SPROUTS SALAD (p. 59)
- ★ Rice
- ★ SWEET POTATOES AND CHESTNUTS (p. 88)

Lunch for six or more

- ★ *MISO* SOUP with *Wakame* seaweed and Scallion (p. 17)
- ★ BEEF BOWL (p. 39)
  or
- ★ *TEMPURA* BOWL (p. 21)
- ★ GREEN BEANS WITH SESAME SEEDS (p. 63)
- ★ Pickles (p. 31)
- ★ Green tea
- ★ Fresh fruit

Dinner for six or more

- ★ FRESH OYSTERS ON THE HALF SHELL (p. 10)
- ★ CLEAR SOUP with Red snapper (p. 14)
- ★ CRAB MEAT SALAD (p. 58)
- ★ *Shabu-shabu* (p. 40)
  or
- ★ LAMB AND VEGETABLES ON GRIDDLE (p. 43)
- ★ SIMMERED *DAIKON* RADISH (p. 67)
- ★ Rice
- ★ Green tea
- ★ SNOW WHITE JELLY (p. 88)

MENU PLANNING

Picnic or Outdoor Party

Main dishes: choose one or two

> ★ *NORI* SEAWEED ROLLED *SUSHI* (p. 74)
> ★ DEEP-FRIED *TOFU* POUCH *SUSHI* (p. 78)
> ★ RICE BALLS (p. 79)
> ★ CHICKEN *TERIYAKI* (p. 32)
> ★ BEEF *TERIYAKI* STEAK (p. 42)

Side dish:

> ★ ROLLED OMELET (p. 49)

Dessert:

> ★ SWEET POTATOES AND CHESTNUTS (p. 88)

The menus given here are merely suggestions. You should feel free to use the recipes in this book in whatever way you like.

When planning a luncheon or a dinner party, set the scene for the party with simple touches, such as suitable background music and/or Japanese flower arrangement.

International atmosphere enhances the mood and the enjoyment of your guests or family.

★ Traditional Presentation (Table setting for one person)

In any course, the meal is followed by green tea and fresh fruit.

Plan A──A meal usually served at home

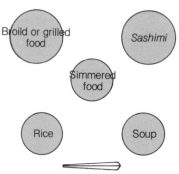

Plan B──A meal served to guests at home

(Proceed from course 1)

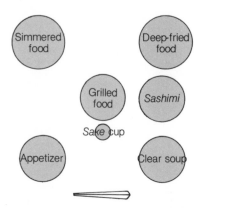
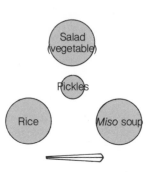

UTENSILS

TRABLEWARE

[Bowls]
① Soup bowl (lacquer ware or plastic ware with or without lid).
② Rice bowl (earthenware, pottery or chinaware)
③ Deep bowls, a little larger than rice bowls (chinaware or lacquer ware) for one-pot dishes or cooked food.

④ Multi-purpose deep bowls come in all sizes. Made of chinaware, earthenware, pottery or glass.
⑤ Large bowl with fitted lid for meat, vegetables or seafood on rice.
⑥ Noodle bowls
⑦ Egg custard cup with lid

[Plates]
① For grilled food (chinaware)
② For *sashimi* (chinaware)
③ For fried food (chinaware or bamboo)
④ For steamed food (chinaware, earthenware, pottery with rim)
⑤ For salad (chinaware, earthen ware, pottery or glass ware)

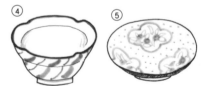

[Miscellaneous]

Bamboo plates or baskets   *Donabe* (earthenware casserole)   Platter

Chopstick rest   Condiment plate or dish   Soy sauce container

UTENSILS

KNIVES

1 All-purpose knife
(Made of stainless steel)

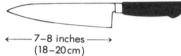

←——— 7–8 inches ———→
(18–20cm)

2 Kitchen cleaver (*deba-bōchō*)
(Made of carbon steel)
This is used for fish, meat and poultry with bones.

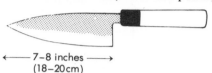

←——— 7–8 inches ———→
(18–20cm)

3 *Sashimi* slicer (*tako-biki*)
(Made of carbon steel)
This is used for slicing fish fillets.

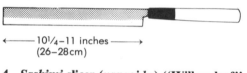

←——— 10¼–11 inches ———→
(26–28cm)

4 *Sashimi* slicer (*yanagi-ba*) "Willow-leaf" slicer
(Made of carbon steel)

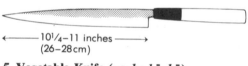

←——— 10¼–11 inches ———→
(26–28cm)

5 Vegetable Knife (*usuba-bōchō*)
(Made of carbon steel)

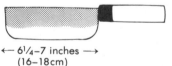

←——— 6¼–7 inches ———→
(16–18cm)

OTHER KNIVES

Kitchen scissors
(Made of stainless steel)

Cheese knife
(Made of carbon steel)

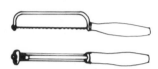

Paring knife
(Made of stainless steel)

Frozen food knife
(Made of stainless steel)

Bread knife
(Made of stainless steel)

★ Knife Sharpening Stone and Knife Sharpener

Knives made of carbon steel should be sharpened with stone. Always wash in hot water and wipe dry with a cloth after using. Moisten stone with water, placing wet cloth or kitchen towel under the stone to secure it. Place the beveled cutting edge of the blade flat on the stone. Push the blade away from you to the edge of the stone. Bring back to start and repeat this stroke with some pressure for 10–20 times and 2–3 times on the other side. All purpose knife should be sharpened with same number of strokes on both sides. Keep your knives sharp.

The beveled cutting edges

correct   wrong   wrong

CHOPPING BOARD

The sharpness of the blade is affected by the chopping board you use. Wood gives the best surface. In Japan, cypress (*hinoki*) seen at *sushi* restaurants is one of the most common materials. Willow or pine is also used. Plastic types are also available. After using, wash it quickly with warm water and wipe dry. To get rid of fishy odors on the chopping board, rub with sliced lemon, lemon juice, vinegar or salt before washing and rinse well. Do not store it while still damp.

CHOPSTICKS (*HASHI*)

They come in various lengths and styles. China, Korea and Vietnam also use chopsticks and each country has different types of chopsticks. Traditional Japanese chopsticks are made of bamboo or cedar. These materials were used so that the fine surface of the pottery would not be scratched and also Japanese like the touch of wood rather than metal. Chopsticks are all-purpose handy utensils for oriental cooks. Use them to reach the bottom of deep pots, pans and bowls and to stir, beat, whisk, turn food and lift all sorts of food.

Today Japanese chopsticks are made of bamboo, cedar, willow, pine, Japanese cypress, (often with a lacquered finish) plastic and metal. Lacquered ones and plastic types are slippery, so it may be best to avoid them. Chopsticks are so useful for any type of cooking that it is worth the effort to learn how to use them. First, place one chopstick in the hollow between the thumb and forefinger and support it on the ring finger. Then, hold the other chopstick with tips of the thumb, forefinger and middle finger and manipulate its tip against the tip of the other one, which is held stationary.

● **Eating chopsticks**——There are three styles of chopsticks available.

    A) *Shojin*-**style:** They are made of Japanese cypress.

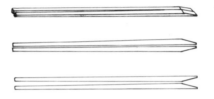

    B) *Rikyu*-**style:** They are of straight-grained cedar. Both ends are pointed. One end for seafood and the other end for meat.

    C) **Disposable type for everyday use:** They are made of bamboo or wood. Disposable chopsticks are practical for everyday use. You can use them several times or throw them away after each use.

Joined pair

Joined at the top, 8 inches (20 cm)

● **Cooking chopsticks**——They are longer than ordinary eating chopsticks, 12 in (30 cm) or longer. Choose the proper length for comfort and ease of handling best suited to you. If you can't find the proper length of chopsticks, simply go out and cut yourself some long and straight twigs and make your own. Pointed chopsticks are the best. You may need to reshape the point by using a sharp knife. Wet the chopsticks before using so that cooking juice will not be absorbed into the chopsticks. Usually they are joined at the top by a piece of string used to hang them when not in use.

● **Serving chopsticks**——These are almost twice as long as eating chopsticks, made of natural wood and with pointed tips.

UTENSILS

BAMBOO or WOODEN SPATULA

This is used for tossing and mixing rice or ingredients.

As it does not break up the rice grains, it is used for serving also. Moisten before use each time.

DROP LID

This is a lightweight wooden lid slightly smaller than the circumference of the cooking pot. In cooking simmered dishes, it is placed directly on top of the ingredients to keep them immersed in the liquid, enabling the flavors to be absorbed.

Always soak the drop-lid in water for a few minutes before using. It absorbs the liquid of the pot and may carry odor. Aluminum foil or heavy butcher-paper is a good substitute for a wooden lid if you can't obtain one. Cut out a circle a little bigger than the pot. A wooden lid can press down on the liquid, but paper may go up and apart from it so fold it up against the sides of the pot.

BAMBOO SKEWERS

For Japanese cooking, bamboo skewers are a very handy tool. They are not only used for many grilled dishes, but to test foods for doneness by pricking and also for cooking raw shrimp; to prevent curling while boiling.

They come in various sizes:

2¾ inch (7 cm) for tooth picks
4¾ inch (12 cm)-short size
6 inch (15 cm)-medium size
7 inch (18 cm)-long size
Longer skewers are also available.

Moisten bamboo skewers before skewering for grilling to prevent breaking or burning. Wash and store them or throw away after one or several uses. Bamboo is a versatile plant; for centuries it's been proven in the Orient. You can use bamboo for various things: houses, furniture, fences, cooking utensils and so on. Bamboo shoot is edible while bamboo leaf is used as a wrapper.

OMELET PAN

This is the Japanese rectangular frying pan for omelet (See page 49). A new omelet pan needs some seasoning by sautèing any vegetable scraps in 2t hot oil. After each use wipe the surface with oil and clean with cloth. This pan is used only for eggs. To clean the corners, wrap the tip of cooking chopstick with paper towel or cloth and remove any bits.

WOK

A wok has many advantages for deep-frying, stir-frying, sautéing and steaming. Because of its large surface area with food moving quickly, the rounded bottom requires a minimum amount of oil, and the slanted sides protects against splattering. To give the wok stability, place the adapter ring over the largest burner, with the side slanting upwards to allow the center of the wok closer proximity to the burner. A newly purchased wok should be given special seasoning. First fill wok ¾ full with water; heat until lukewarm. Add detergent and scrub well with a brush. Repeat. Cut-up half an onion into slices. Heat 2 t oil in the wok until hot over high heat. Add onion slices and stir-fry rotating wok constantly to coat sloping sides until onion slices are almost burnt to black. Discard the onion and oil. Wash the wok with hot water and dry. Whenever the wok is used for steaming, it must be reseasoned afterward in order to prevent food from sticking. The cover and steaming rack are for steaming food. A steaming rack, made of metal is used to elevate plates of food above the boiling water in wok while steaming. Special Japanese steamers are available, but unless a lot of food is steamed, a wok with steaming rack and cover is sufficient.

CAST-IRON POT and PAN

This is a round cast-iron pan used for cooking *sukiyaki*, and for one-pot dishes cooking meat or fish with vegetables. A new cast-iron pan needs seasoning. Scrub it in water, then fill it with water until almost full and bring to the boil. Discard the boiling water. Repeat 2–3 times to remove the protective oil applied when manufactured. Dry thoroughly. Then heat ½ cup used oil in the pan and sauté some vegetable scraps until all vegetables are tender. Discard the vegetable scraps. Fill pan with water and bring to the boil. Rinse and repeat. Dry thoroughly or over moderate heat and rub a dab of oil on the inside surface to prevent rusting. If rust appears, simply scrub clean and re-season. But, never scour your pot with coarse grained cleansers. Electric Teflon coated skillet or wok is a good substitute. They are especially suited for entertaining or cooking at the table.

DEEP-FRYING THERMOMETER

This handy device will ensure the exact oil temperature in recipes calling for deep-frying, *tempura*, pork cutlet and so on.

UTENSILS

LACQUER WARE

For serving foods lacquer ware is used in Japanese cooking. New ones have some odor, so wipe them with vinegar, using lint free soft cloth. Leave it in well ventilated dark place. Do not use dish soap. Avoid prolonged soaking in hot or cold water. To retain beautiful glossy shine, dab on a bit of oil with cotton and wipe off thoroughly with a soft cloth. Be careful not to scratch them with finger nails or ring. To store wrap with tissue paper. Do not put in the dishwasher.

DONABE (EARTHENWARE CASSEROLE)

The *donabe* is made from special clay and can be used directly over the flame. Conventional oven-proof-ware like stoneware can never be put on direct heat. However, the Japanese *donabe* can be used in an oven as well. It retains heat well and distributes heat evenly. These are great advantages when cooking at the table.

The *donabe* comes in small one-portion size: 7 inch (18cm), in medium size: 10 inch (25cm), in large sizes: 12 inch (30cm). The lid of a donabe is always glazed inside and out. The inside of the body is glazed but not the outside. For first time use, fill it with water and a pinch of salt and boil over moderate heat for 5 minutes. Before putting it on a burner the unglazed outside must be completely dry and it should not be put empty on a flame. In case it cracks, cook gruel rice (*okayu*) in it. The small cracks will be sealed by gruel rice. Despite its heavy appearance, a *donabe* is very fragile, so knocks and bumps should be avoided. When putting in a dishwasher, be careful so that it will not jiggle against other pots and pans.

JAPANESE GRINDING BOWL and PESTLE

The Japanese grinding bowl is a pottery bowl serrated on the inside. It comes in various sizes. The pestle is made of wood and also comes in various lengths. To clean the bowl, use the tip of a bamboo skewer to loosen any hard bits that stick in the bowl's grooves. Wash with a stiff brush under running water.

HANGIRI (WOODEN MIXING TUB)

This is used for mixing cooked rice with vinegar flavoring. Professional *sushi* cooks use cypress tubs. However, a large, plastic or enamel or glass bowl will do just as well.

MAKISU (BAMBOO MAT)

Narrow strips of bamboo are held together by cotton string. *Makisu* is used for shaping soft ingredients such as *NORI* SEAWEED ROLLED *SUSHI* (see page 74) and ROLLED OMELET (see page 49).

HOW TO USE BAMBOO MAT

WOODEN MOLD

This wooden mold is used to make pressed *sushi*. The mold consists of three pieces, like a large oriental puzzle. If you make *sushi* often, a wooden mold is useful, but not essential. Instead of the mold, use a pan with a removable bottom, a stainless spring-form pan, or if you have utensils for French cooking, you can innovate. Make your own mold with a stainless form pan. Be sure to wet the mold before adding rice.

INGREDIENTS

ATSUAGE (deep-fried *tofu*)·
ABURAGE (deep-fried *tofu* pouch)

Atsuage is deep-fried regular *tofu*. It is fried until the outside becomes crisp and golden brown but the inside is still white. *Aburage* is also deep-fried *tofu*, but before frying it is cut into thin sheets.

BAMBOO SHOOTS

Bamboo shoots are one of the most common ingredients in Asian cooking. In Japan, bamboo shoots are "cooked-fresh", canned in water and available all year-round. Occasionally, such water-packed bamboo is exported and available in U.S..

BEAN THREADS

These are long, dry noodles made of mung bean flour. They keep on the shelf indefinitely. Soak them in warm water for 15 min before use. They may also be deep-fried in hot oil. Do not soak them in water prior to deep-frying though. Use them as a noodle in soups, or with stir fried vegetables and meat. To keep them as clean as possible place them in a large paper bag before removing wrapper. Break off amount needed and store remainder in bag.

CHINESE CABBAGE

This versatile, greenish-white leafed cabbage is used in stir-fry and one-pot dishes. It is also added to soups, and made into pickles. A heavy, succulent vegetable, Chinese cabbage is often found in supermarkets, not to mention oriental food stores. It is also known as "celery cabbage" and "nappa (sometimes 'Napa') cabbage." Avoid produce with spotted leaves, if possible. Store as you would lettuce.

DAIKON RADISH

Daikon radish is rich in vitamins, and its leaves contain much calcium. This radish is thought to aid in the digestion of oily foods. It is good for simmered dishes.

DRIED BONITO

This is an important ingredient in *dashi* stock. A stick of dried bonito looks like a 6–8 in (15–20 cm) long brownish hunk of wood.

Shaved, dried bonito flakes are also available in packs and convenient to use.

Dried bonito "thread" shavings are often used as a garnish. Such "thread" shavings look like rosy-beige excelsior and have a pleasant flavor. If you cannot obtain them, use regular dried bonito flakes.

DRIED *WAKAME* SEAWEED

This seaweed is usually sold in dried form. *Wakame* seaweed can be used for various soups. It is also a good salad ingredient. It should not be simmered more than a minute. *Wakame* seaweed is rich in vitamins and proteins.

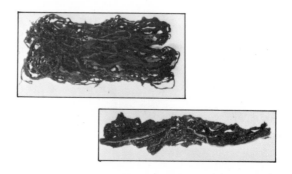

EGGPLANTS

Eggplants used here are the 6 in (15 cm) variety that weigh approximately 10 oz (285 g) each, rather than the small Japanese eggplants that are on the average 4 in (10 cm) long and weigh 2–3 oz (60–90 g). Because size varies with region and season, weights have been included to offer a guideline. If using the small Japanese variety, substitute 3–4 eggplants in these recipes, again using the listed weight as a guide.

ENOKITAKE MUSHROOMS

Enokitake mushrooms are mild-flavored and have a pleasant crispness and aroma. They are often used in soups. There are canned *enokitake* mushrooms but fresh ones are better.

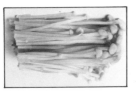

GANMODOKI

Ganmodoki consists of crumbled *tofu*, sesame seeds, ginkgo nuts and slivered vegetables like carrots, mushrooms, and burdock bound together with grated mountain yam. This *tofu*-based mixture is formed into 3 in (8 cm) patties or 1½ in (4 cm) balls, then deep-fried. They are used in simmered dishes. They go well with soy sauce.

GINGER ROOT

Choose ginger root that is firm and tight. Avoid pieces that are flabby or have soft spots. Pare skin of amount you will use.

GRILLED *TOFU*

Grilled *tofu* is called *yaki-dofu* in Japanese. Grilled *tofu* has been grilled on both sides over charcoal, thus producing its firm texture. It is easy to recognize by the light mottling on the skin. If *yaki-dofu* is not available, you can make it easily. Drain regular *tofu* and lightly grill each side of *tofu* over high heat. Grilled *tofu* is often used in boiled dishes such as *Sukiyaki*.

JAPANESE CUCUMBER

Recipes in this book call for American cucumbers, which are equivalent to 2 or 3 Japanese cucumbers. In general, peel and seed cucumbers unless skin is delicate and thin and seeds are immature. If using the small Japanese variety, it is not necessary to peel or seed. However to smooth the rough surface and to bring out the skin color, dredge the cucumber in salt and roll it back and forth on a cutting board using the palm of your hand. Wash well.

JAPANESE HOT PEPPER

Red pepper is used fresh or dried. Dried and ground coarse pepper is called *ichimi*, or one flavor spice. This *ichimi* is one of the component ingredients of *shichimi* or seven-spice mixture. *Shichimi* is a collection of seven dried and ground flavors: red pepper flakes; roughly ground, brown *sanshō* pepper pods; minute flakes of dried dark green *nori* seaweed bits; and white sesame seeds.

INGREDIENTS

KAMABOKO·CHIKUWA (Steamed fish paste)

Kamaboko is made mainly from fish protein. Good *kamaboko* is white and elastic and the cut end is glossy. Keep in refrigerator. *Chikuwa* literally means ring of bamboo. Both *kamaboko* and *chikuwa* go well with horseradish soy sauce.

KAMPYO

Kampyo is dried gourd shavings. It is used as one of the fillings for rolled *sushi*. To soften, first wash then knead strips for one use in an ample amount of salt. Wash in water, then boil until soft. It is available in 1oz (30g) package.

KOMBU (KELP)

Kombu is one of the basic ingredients used for making *dashi* stock. When you use it, never wash or rinse. The speckled surface of the kelp holds flavor, so do not wash. Kelp contains the most iodine of all seaweeds.

KONNYAKU·ITO-KONNYAKU

Konnyaku, made from the roots of "devil's tongue" has no calories. It must be simmerd for a long time before eating. *Ito-konnyaku* is *konnyaku* strips.

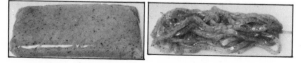

KŌYA-DOFU (freeze-dried *tofu*)

This is made from soybeans. One package usually contains five to six pieces. It looks like a beige sponge and is very light. Prior to cooking, it should be soaked in lukewarm water until soft. It will double the volume. It is easily simmered and it goes well with soy sauce. Freeze dried *tofu* was originally a daily food for monks in Japan. Now it is popular with everyone.

LOTUS ROOT

The flesh is white and "crunchy". Long tubular hollows run through the entire length of the root. When preparing lotus root for cooking, pare it first. Then cut into rounds. The shape should be attractive. To prevent discoloring it should be immersed for a short time in a mixture of alum and water or  vinegar and water. This also gets rid of any harshness in flavor. It can then be boiled in water containing a little vinegar. It goes well with vinegared dishes.

MIRIN

Mirin is heavily sweetened *sake*, used for cooking. *Mirin* is called "sweet cooking rice wine." *Sake* sweetened with sugar can be a substituted.

INGREDIENTS

MISO

Miso is fermented soybean paste. The colors range from yellow to brown; yellow *miso* is referred to as *shiro miso* in this book. Brown *miso* is called *aka miso*. Since there are various kinds of *miso*, it might be helpful to learn about *miso* by buying small quantities of various kinds. It is used for soups, dressings, sauces, etc.

NATTŌ

This is a fermented soybean preparation made by the action of special bacteria. It has a rich cheese-like flavor

and is sticky. With good *nattō,* the sticky "threads" formed while mixing should be strong and stubborn and the beans should be moderately moist.

NIBOSHI

Niboshi is made from small sardines. These are soft-boned fish which are sun-dried. They are used for fish stock. The fish stock has rather a strong flavor and it is used for *miso* soup or noodle broth.

NORI SEAWEED

The best quality *nori* seaweed is glossy black-purple. It is used after toasting which improves flavor and texture. *Nori* seaweed grows around bamboo stakes placed under water. When the time comes, it is gathered, washed, laid in thin sheets and dried. It contains lots of protein.

OKARA

Okara is a by-product of the *tofu*-making process. It looks like moist, white, crumbly saw dust. It is a delight to make various dishes with this high-protein, low-calorie food, *okara*.

SAKE

Sake is made by inoculating steamed mold (*kōji*) and then allowing fermentation to occur. It is then refined it. In Japan *sake* is the most popular beverage, but it is also used in various ways in cooking.

SANSHŌ, KINOME SPRIGS

Both the leaves and seed pods of *sanshō* are used. Dried leaves are powdered and used as a spice, *sansho* pepper. The young leaves, called *kinome* sprigs are mainly used to garnish foods.

SESAME OIL

Made from sesame seeds which are rich in oil and protein, this oil has a unique taste and aroma. It is mixed with salad oil and used for frying *tempura* or used to add flavor and aroma to the dressing used on Japanese-style *aemono* dishes.

INGREDIENTS

SESAME SEEDS

Both black and white sesame seeds are used in Japanese cooking. When toasted, sesame seeds have a much richer flavor. Richer still however, are ground sesame seeds. To grind sesame seeds use a *suribachi* (Japanese grinding bowl). Before grinding, toast seeds in a dry frying pan. It is a nice garnish.

SHICHIMI-TŌGARASHI (7-SPICE POWDER)

This is a good spice for sprinkling over *Udon*, *Mizutaki*, etc. Because it loses its aroma quickly, buy it in small quantities and store, tightly covered.

SHIITAKE MUSHROOMS

Both fresh and dried *shiitake* mushrooms can be obtained. Dried ones should be soaked in water before using. This soaking water makes *dashi* stock (Japanese soup stock). Fresh *shiitake* mushroom have a distinctive, appealing "woody-fruity" flavor. *Shiitake* mushroom are good for simmered dishes because of their special flavor. The best one have thick, brown velvety caps and firm flesh.

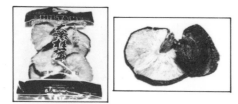

SHISO LEAVES

These minty, aromatic leaves come in green and red varieties. The red type is used to make *umeboshi* (pickled plum).

SOYBEANS

Soybeans were one of the "five sacred grains" of ancient China. They have many cultivars including black and yellow ones and countless uses: they can be used in stews, turned into soy paste, soy milk, also *tofu*, and can be used as a meat substitute.

SOY SAUCE

Soy sauce is made from soybeans, and salt. It is the primary seasoning of Japanese cooking. It is used for simmered foods, dressings, soups; many kinds of Japanese dishes. Ordinary soy sauce is dark, but one which has a light color is also available. The light soy sauce does not darken the colors of food, and it is salty enough. Thick soy sauce is a good seasoning for raw fish, *Sashimi*. It is rather sweet.

TOFU

Tofu, "bean curd" in English, is an important product of soybeans. It is rich in proteins, vitamins, and minerals. It is low in calories and saturated fats, and entirely free of cholesterol.

There are two kinds of *tofu*: cotton *tofu* and silk *tofu*. Cotton *tofu* is firm. Silk *tofu* is softer and contains more whey.

INGREDIENTS

TREFOIL (*MITSUBA*)

Trefoil is a member of the parsley family. The flavor is somewhere between sorrel and celery. It accents the flavor of many Japanese dishes.

UMEBOSHI

Umeboshi are made every June when green plums come onto the market in Japan. Green, unripe plums are soaked in brine, packed with red *shiso* leaves and left to mature in the salty bath. In Japan *umeboshi* have long been regarded as a tonic. Not only are they thought to help in digestion, but they also keep the intestinal tract clear. This may be one of the reasons why *umeboshi* are served with the traditional Japanese breakfast. Also *umeboshi* paste can be a seasoning.

VINEGAR

Japanese rice vinegar is milder than most Western vinegars. Lightness and relative sweetness are characteristics of rice vinegar. Use cider vinegar rather than anything synthetic if substituting.

VINEGARED FRESH GINGER

5–6 stalks young fresh ginger
Vinegar Mixture:
    ½ cup vinegar
    4 tablespoons sugar
    1 teaspoon salt
    ½ cup water

Bring Vinegar Mixture to the boil. Cool. Pour mixture into a glass. Cut leaves off fresh ginger, leaving about 9 in (23 cm) of stem. Clean roots. Dip only the roots into boiling salted water. Remove immediately. Shake off water. Dip in Vinegar Mixture while hot.

WASABI

Wasabi is Japanese horseradish. It is pale green in color. It has a more delicate aroma and is milder tasting than Western horseradish. In Japan both fresh and powdered *wasabi* are available, but it is hard to obtain fresh *wasabi* in other countries. The edible part of *wasabi* is the root. Usually it comes in a powdered form or in a tube, but the fragrance of fresh *wasabi* is much richer than powdered *wasabi*. The powder should be mixed with water to make a thick paste. *Wasabi* accompanies most raw fish dishes, and also *Sushi*. Raw fish may be hard to try for the first time, but with the added taste of soy sauce and *wasabi*, it will become one of your favorites.

YUZU CITRON

Japanese citron. The fragrant rind is grated and added as a garnish to soups and other dishes. This citrus fruit appears also in Chinese and Korean cooking. In the West where *yuzu* citron is not often available, lemon or lime rind or zest can be used though neither is quite the same.

METRIC TABLES

Today many areas of the world use the metric system and more will follow in the future. The following conversion tables are intented as a guide to help you.

General points of information that may prove valuable or of interest:
1 British fluid ounce = 28.5 ml
1 American fluid ounce = 29.5 ml

1 Japanese cup = 200 ml
1 British cup = 200 ml = 7 British fl oz
1 American cup = 240 ml = 8 American fl oz

1 British pint = 570 ml = 20 British fl oz
1 American pint = 470 ml = 16 American fl oz
T = tablespoon   oz = ounce   g = gram   ml = milliliter

Weights

ounces to grams	grams to ounces
$1/4$ oz = 7 g	1 g = 0.035 oz
$1/2$ oz = 14 g	5 g = $1/6$ oz
1 oz = 30 g	10 g = $1/3$ oz
2 oz = 60 g	28 g $\doteqdot$ 1 oz
4 oz = 115 g	100 g = $3 1/2$ oz
6 oz = 170 g	200 g = 7 oz
8 oz = 225 g	500 g = 18 oz
16 oz = 450 g	1000 g = 35 oz

grams × 0.035 = ounces
ounces × 28.35 = grams

Linear Measures

inches to centimeters	centimeters to inches
$1/2$ in = 1.27 cm	1 cm = $3/8$ in
1 in = 2.54 cm	2 cm = $3/4$ in
2 in = 5.08 cm	3 cm = $1 1/8$ in
4 in = 10.16 cm	4 cm = $1 1/2$ in
5 in = 12.7 cm	5 cm = 2 in
10 in = 25.4 cm	10 cm = 4 in
15 in = 38.1 cm	15 cm = $5 3/4$ in
20 in = 50.8 cm	20 cm = 8 in

inches × 2.54 = centimeters
centimeters × 0.39 = inches

in = inch   cm = centimeter

Temperatures

Fahrenheit (F) to Celsius (C)		Celsius (C) to Fahrenheit (F)	
freezer storage	−10°F = −23.3°C	freezer storage	−20°C = −4°F
	0°F = −17.7°C		−10°C = 14°F
water freezes	32°F = 0 °C	water freezes	0°C = 32°F
	68°F = 20 °C		10°C = 50°F
	100°F = 37.7°C		50°C = 122°F
water boils	212°F = 100 °C	water boils	100°C = 212°F
	300°F = 148.8°C		150°C = 302°F
	400°F = 204.4°C		200°C = 392°F

The water boiling temperature given is at sea level.

Conversion factors:
$$C = F - 32 \times 5/9$$
$$F = \frac{C \times 9}{5} + 32$$

C = Celsius   F = Fahrenheit

INDEX

Japanese foods sponsored by Nishimoto Trading Co., Ltd.

NTC NISHIMOTO TRADING CO., LTD.

LOS ANGELES
1111, MATEO ST., LOS ANGELES, CALIF. 90021
TEL: (213) 689-9330

SAN FRANCISCO
410 EAST GRAND AVE., SO. SAN FRANCISCO, CALIF. 94080
TEL: (415) 871-2490

NEW YORK
21-23, EMPIRE BLVD., SOUTH HACKENSACK, NEW JERSEY 07606
TEL; (212) 349-0056

HONOLULU
NISHIMOTO TRADING CO., HAWAII, LTD.
537 KAAAHI ST., P.O. BOX 636 HONOLULU, HAWAII 96809
TEL: (808) 848-0761/847-1354

DÜSSELDORF
BEETHOVENSTR 19. 4000 DUSSELDORF 1, WEST GER-MANY
TEL: (0211) 660884

OFFICES IN JAPAN.
KOBE OFFICE:
2-11 KAIGANDORI 3-CHOME, CHUO-KU, KOBE 650
TEL: (078)391-6911

TOKYO OFFICE:
2-14, 3-CHOME, SOTOKANDA, CHIYODA-KU, TOKYO 101
TEL: (03) 253-5221

NAHA OFFICE:
1-9, 1-CHOME, MATSUYAMA-CHO, NAHA, OKINAWA 900
TEL: (0988) 68-1136